Table of Co

I am nothing
I'll never be anything
I couldn't want to be something
Apart from that, I have in me
all the dreams in the world

Alvaro de Campos. Tabacaria

ZEN WAY OF SEEING

Fernando Pessoa (1888—1935) was a famous Portuguese poet, writer, political commentator, philosopher, astrologer and mystic. He is mostly known for creation of his own poetic universe, consisting of over 70 heteronyms, which are imaginary characters with their own separate, yet interacting with each other, lives. Pessoa endowed them with their own poetic style, handwriting and even personal horoscopes. The most famous of them are Alberto Caeiro, Ricardo Reis, Alvaro de Campos and Bernardo Soares. There is even a joke, that there are four great poets in Portugal — all of them Pessoa. Some critics compared him to «octopus-poet», with heteronyms like so many tentacles. It can be said, that although imaginary, Pessoa's heteronyms, based on the fact that people still discuss them hundred years later, are more real than their actual contemporaries, who passed away without any trace. It is ironic in that regard, that Pessoa in Portuguese means «Person», yet he had no person of his own, since it was replaced with that of his heteronyms.

Although he was already recognized during his life, most of his work, especially that of his heteronyms, was published after his death in

1935. Pessoa left about 25000 sheets of manuscripts in his large trunk, which is now located at the Portuguese National Library. He became popular first in Brazil, then his work was translated into French and English, and then his fame skyrocketed in the 80's after publication of his «Book of Disquiet» (authored by semi-heteronym Bernardo Soares), which Pessoa considered as his «factless autobiography» and which was translated into multiple languages.

After so many books published about Fernando Pessoa, especially after Richard Zenith's thousand page biography «Pessoa»[1], one might ask what else could be written about Pessoa. Yet, in Richard Zenith's tour de force we encounter a statement that somewhat indicates a misunderstanding of what was Pessoa's actual spiritual state: «Pessoa, of course, never achieved anything remotely resembling Zen Buddhist enlightenment»[2]. He comes to this conclusion, despite noticing a lot of similarities in Caeiro's poetry to Zen koans[3]. The goal of this work is to prove otherwise, and show that Pessoa has actually achieved highest levels of

---

[1] R. Zenith, Pessoa: A Biography. 2021

[2] Ibid

[3] R.Zenith. Alberto Caeiro as Zen heteronym

nondual awareness, which is the goal of Zen.

The «Zen quality» of Pessoa's poetry, especially that of Alberto Caeiro, was first observed by an American trappist monk Thomas Merton, who was a writer, poet, theologian, mystic and scholar of comparative religion himself, much like Pessoa. Intellectually, Merton was heavily influenced by Rene Guenon, a French intellectual, converted to Islam and founder of the Traditionalist school, specializing in initiation, symbolism, eastern religions and sacred science. Poetically, Merton aspired after Pessoa's Alberto Caeiro. In fact, Merton was the first one to translate twelve Caeiro poems from the «Keeper of the sheep» into English in order to demonstrate to Zen master and propagandist in the West Dr. Suzuki that the «Zen quality» was known in Europe long before Zen became widespread. Merton said, that «Pessoa-Caeiro may be numbered among those Western writers who have expressed something akin to the Zen way of seeing things — «the knack of full awareness»[4].

This «Zen way of seeing things» is a way of seeing things from the perspective of nondual awareness and it will be discussed in the second

[4] Ibid

part of the book. A lot of people, like Merton and other scholars, were able to feel it, yet since they were always looking from the perspective of duality, they were not able to adequately describe Pessoa's phenomenology or his way of seeing things. It takes one to know one. The goal of this work is to provide the complete framework necessary for understating Pessoa's vision, which is that of nondual awareness, and is the key to all his poetry.

Although not aware of Zen at his time, since it was gaining its recognition in the West much later, Pessoa owned several hundred books on all sorts of esoterism, like Astrology, Hermeticism, Theosophy, Alchemy, Kabbala, Rosicrucianism and Freemasonry. He also abundantly wrote on those matters himself. In 1915–16 Pessoa translated several books by theosophical authors like Annie Besant, Helena Blavatsky, and some others, but later he became disillusioned with their teachings. The same topics were also of special interest for Rene Guenon, who, similarly, started his path in occultist circles and later published their scathing criticism in his two books, «Spiritist fallacy» and «Theosophy: a history of a pseudo-religion». It is interesting that, despite Pessoa's interest in occult and even acquaintance with Aleister Crowley, he was unaware of Guenon, although they were contemporaries. Some overlap between the two will be addressed in the first part of the book. Also, Guenon's theory of multiple states of the being, expounded in his book under the same title, will be used to explain Pessoa's heteronym phenomenon.

Based on his esoteric studies, Pessoa broke down initiation onto several steps, that of neophyte, magician, mystic, alchemist and master. In this work, we will try to isolate the main poetic theme of each major Pessoa heteronym, and show how these themes roughly corresponds to those initiation steps as well as to the different stages of nondual awareness. In the end, we will show how they can be used as keys for understanding Western Philosophy, Christianity and Yoga.

INITIATION

PESSOA

According to Hermetism, Hermes gave people three sciences: astrology, alchemy and magic. Pessoa had studied and explored all of them. Being an avid astrologer, he had cast hundreds of horoscopes for historical figures (like King Sebastian, Napoleon, Mussolini, Hitler), literature authors (Shakespeare, Milton, Goethe, Byron, Oscar Wilde), his friends, himself, and his heteronyms. He did not really believe in stars per se, but he believed in the Destiny, which can be represented in the stars:

> What operates on us is a destiny, and that destiny, which exists as a spiritual force on a higher plane, is materially, or cosmologically, represented in the stars[5].

In fact, this is how Pessoa got acquainted with English occultist and poet Aleister Crowley, as he discovered some inaccuracies in Crowley horoscopes and asked his publisher to inform him about it:

> If you have occasion to communicate, as you probably have, with Mr. Aleister Crowley, you

---

[5] R Zenith, The Selected Prose of Fernando Pessoa

> may inform him that his horoscope is unrectified, and that if he reckons himself as born at 11h.16m.39s. p.m. on the 12th. October 1875, he will have Aries 11 as his midheaven, with the corresponding ascendant and cusps. He will then find his directions more exact than he has probably found them hitherto. This is a mere speculation, of course, and I am sorry to inflict upon you this purely fantastic intrusion into what is, after all, only a business letter[6].

They have met in Lisbon in September of 1930. There is a picture of them playing chess. To boost his publicity, Crowley with the help of Pessoa performed a stunt with a fake suicide at the Boca do Inferno, known for its high cliffs over the ocean. Pessoa reported him missing to the police, but after three weeks Crowley reappeared in Berlin at the opening of his art exhibition at the Gallery Neumann-Nierendorf. This gave rise to a number of speculations about his association with Hitler. Rene Guenon describes it in detail in the letter to Julius Evola from 29 October 1949:

> To come back to Aleister Crowley, what you told me reminds me of the story that turned up in 1931 (I believe at least that was the exact date): while he was in Portugal, he

[6] Marco Pasi, Aleister Crowley and the Temptation of Politics.

> suddenly disappeared. They found his clothes on the border of the sea, something that made them believe he had drowned. But it was only a simulated death, since they were no longer concerned about him and did not try to find out where he had gone. Actually, he went to Berlin to play the role of secret adviser to Hitler who was then at his beginning. It is probably this that had given rise to certain tales about the Golden Dawn, but in reality it was only about Crowley, because it does not seem that a certain English colonel named Etherton, who was then his «colleague», had ever had the least relationship with that organisation. A little later, Crowley founded the Saturn-Lodge in Germany; have you ever heard of it? There he called himself Master Therion, and his signature was «to mega Therion» (the Great Beast), something that in Greek gives exactly the numeric value 666[7].

Crowley association with Hitler was never confirmed. Aleister Crowley was a member of Golden Dawn, along with other famous people of the time like Sir Arthur Conan Doyle, Gustav Meyrink, Bram Stoker, W.B. Yeats. Later, Crowley broke up with the order and published its secret teachings in order to democratize the magic, making it available to anyone. Then, he joined an Ordo Templi Orientis, and, in fact, his

[7] Guenon.Letter to Evola X

visit to Lisbon had its goal to establish its Portuguese headquarters, which supposedly would be led by Pessoa.

This brings the questions of whether Pessoa was initiated into any esoteric organization. Rene Guenon spoke of regular and irregular initiation. Regular initiation is essentially a horizontal initiation through the initiation rite by attaching neophyte to the Initiatory chain, which channels Divine influences. That's basically initiation into some organization, like Freemasonry etc. Irregular initiation is more of an anomaly, and happens to a person directly and vertically, «from above», often without attachment to any organization.

Similarly to Guenon, Pessoa considered the regular initiation as a path of the right hand, which can be either exoteric or esoteric, and irregular initiation as a path of the left hand, Divine initiation:

> Exoteric initiate is, for example, any Freemason, or any minor disciple of a theosophical or anttroposophical society. Esoteric Initiate is, for example, a Rosicrucian, a Francis Bacon. Divine Initiate is, for example, a Shakespeare. This type of initiation is commonly called genius[8].

So, genius is a form of penetration into invisible realities, talking to angels, as Pessoa reflects elsewhere:

> The man of genius is an initiate of the left hand. Shakespeare. He is one initiate who feels but does not know his initiation. (...) To be initiated is to be admitted to talk of angels. Some hear, others see and hear. The first ones are on the left, the others on the right[9].

With respect to regular initiation, Pessoa wrote in 1935 that he was «initiated, through direct communication from Master to Disciple, into the three lesser degrees of the (apparently extinct) Templar Order of Portugal». It is known that on September 9, 1930 Crowley initiated Pessoa's friend Raul Leal into Ordo Templi Orientis. Marco Pasi confirmed in his study that Pessoa was most likely present in the room, and since outsiders should be precluded from the rite, this means that he was either already initiated or became initiated at the same time. A private note by Pessoa discovered in the new Pessoa-Crowley correspondence reads:

> To feel the opposition of the middle is the beginning of the impulse toward victory. This was given to me by the Master Therion with

---

[8] Espólio de Fernando Pessoa. Esp. 125A-8

[9] Esp. 54B-20

> authorization from above. Creating a disanalogy between myself and the one who encircles me: this is the first step and the beginning of the awakening[10].

Here, Pessoa refers to Crowley as Master Therion, thus recognizing his spiritual authority, while previously in the correspondence he was addressing him as a brother. Some find this claim of initiation speculative, since in a different letter to Adolfo Casais Monteiro from January 1935 Pessoa said:

> As to «initiation» or lack thereof, I can tell you only this, for I do not know how to answer your question: I do not belong to any Initiatory Order. The quote, the epigraph to my poem Eros e Psique, from a passage (translated, since the Ritual is in Latin) of the Ritual of the Third Degree of the Templar Order of Portugal, indicates simply — this is a fact — that I was permitted to leaf through the Rituals of the first three degrees of this Order, which has been extinct or dormant since circa 1888. Were it not dormant, I would not have quoted this part of the Ritual, because one must not quote passages (indicating the source) from rituals that are being used[11].

Despite the presence or absence of regular

---

[10] Marco Pasi, Aleister Crowley and the Temptation of Politics.

[11] Ibid

initiation, we can state that he most definitely received irregular initiation, as a result of which he transitioned from perspective of duality into nondual awareness. Since this transition is a shocking event, mostly like it occurred at the moment of creations of his first three heteronyms, which left on him the most vivid impression, as he describes in a famous letter to Adolfo Casais Monteiro:

> One day when I'd finally given up — it was March 8th, 1914—I walked over to a high chest of drawers, took a sheet of paper, and began to write standing up, as I do whenever I can. And I wrote thirty-some poems at once, in a kind of ecstasy I'm unable to describe. It was the triumphal day of my life, and I can never have another one like it. I began with a title, The Keeper of Sheep. This was followed by the appearance in me of someone whom I instantly named Alberto Caeiro. Excuse the absurdity of this statement: my master had appeared in me[12].

Right away we notice the mention of the states of giving up and indescribable ecstasy, that he never had anything like it and that it was the most triumphant day of his life. These are clear signs of Divine initiation, which is then confirmed with giving Alberto Caeiro the title of

---

[12] R.Zenith. Pessoa; A Biography

master, which he also applied to Crowley. Pessoa most likely considered it an initiation himself as he was extensively elaborating on the poetry as a means of initiation. In the end, in the autobiographic note written eight months before his death, Pessoa identified himself as gnostic Christian:

> Gnostic Christian, and therefore entirely opposed to all organized Churches, and above all to the Church of Rome. Faithful, for reasons which are implied below, to Secret Tradition of Christianity, which has close relations with the Secret Tradition in Israel (the Holy Kabala) and with the hidden essence of Freemasonry.

TWO ABYSSES

«Know thyself» is the ultimate maxim of Western Esotericism. The questions is, which self it had in mind. The main outcome of Pessoa contacts with theosophical literature, which happened early in his adulthood and lasted throughout his life, was the belief in the Higher reality and Higher Self, which is radically different from the ego or the ordinary self. Pessoa writes: «Creating a disanalogy between myself and the one who encircles me: this is the first step and the beginning of the awakening»[13]. Here, the «one who encircles me» is the Higher Self or the «Spirit of the Soul», which is different from ego (Soul), hence the realization of disanalogy between ego and Higher Soul:

> The Spirit of our Soul, being our substance, is nevertheless distinct from us in this world and is someone else.

By using the word «encircling» Pessoa alludes to the circle as the symbol of both worlds. Ouroboros, or snake biting its tail, is the «symbol of the earth or of the world such as it is». Then, there is also the circle of Higher reality. Both circles symbolize the infinity of the abyss. Bernardo Soares writes his famous

---

[13] Marco Pasi, Aleister Crowley and the Temptation of Politics

description of the soul abyss:

> My soul is a black whirlpool, a vast vertigo circling a void, the racing of an infinite ocean around a hole in nothing. And in these waters which are more a churning than actual waters float the images of all I've seen and heard in the world — houses, faces, books, boxes, snatches of music and syllables of voices all moving in a sinister and bottomless swirl.
>
> And amid all this confusion I, what's truly I, am the center that exists only in the geometry of the abyss: I'm the nothing around which everything spins, existing only so that it can spin, being a center only because every circle has one. I, what's truly I, am a well without walls but with the walls' viscosity, the center of everything with nothing around it[14].

Or, as Pessoa poetically put it in «Marytime Ode»:

> The feverish machine of my teeming visions
> Now spins at such frightening, inordinate speed
> That my flywheel consciousness
> Is just a blurry circle whirring in the air.[15]

This Higher reality is the only true reality, which means that the visible world, reality we are

---

[14] Pessoa. Book of Disquite, 262. Translated by R.Zenith.

[15] Patrícia Silva McNeill. Sacred Geometry of Being: Pessoa's Esoteric Imagery and the Geometry of Modernism

living in, is an illusion or a sleep from which one must awaken. The transition from illusion of this world to reality of the Higher Self is the goal of initiation:

> Initiation means in reality that this very visible world where we live in is symbol and shadow, that this life we know through our senses is death and sleep, or so to say, that what we see is all but an illusion. Initiation casts away, gradually, partially, this illusion. It keeps its path secret because most human beings are not prepared to understand it and would create misunderstanding, havoc and confusion if it were made available to the general public. It is symbolic because it is not about knowledge but about life, and that man must decipher all by himself what the symbols presents, as he will live their life and will not content himself just to learn the words that manifest them[16].

The lower world is manifested world, while the higher world is occult world, but both worlds are illusory. Pessoa writes in the «Way of Serpent»:

> Illusion is the substance of the world and as such, according to the Law, it is both in the upper world and in the lower world, both in the occult and in the manifesto. Thus, when we flee from the lower world because it is illusory, the higher world in which we take

---

[16] Pessoa. On initiation

> refuge is no less illusory; it is illusory in another way, one's own. Only the Snake, by surrounding the open infinites — or the «**incomplete**» circles — of the two worlds, escapes the illusion and knows the principle of truth[17].

This transition from one world to the other or from one circle to the other is symbolized by the snake tracing bottom half circle into the upper half circle. The snake with its S shape surrounds both worlds symbolized by circles. Circle is the symbol of this lower world such as it is, «the snake biting its tail», and of the higher world, the Zodiac Circle. In the lower world snake has a shape of crescent moon, in the upper world a shape of a waning moon. «In its S shape, the Snake escapes from the two Realities and disappears from the Worlds and Universes».

Pessoa's heteronym Alexander Search in his English poem «Circle» also writes about incomplete or imperfect circles:

> I traced a circle on the ground,
> It was a mystic figure strange
> Wherein I thought there would abound
> Mute symbols adequate of change,
> And complex formulas of Law,
> Which is the jaws of Change's maw.

---

[17] Pessoa. Way of Serpent

My simpler thoughts in vain had stemmed
The current of this madness free,
But that my thinking is condemned
To symbol and analogy:
I deemed a circle might condense
With calm all mystery's violence.
And so in cabalistic mood
A circle traced I curious there;
Imperfect the made circle stood
Thought formed with minutest care.
From magic's failure deeply I
A lesson took to make me sigh[18].

Imperfect circle is literary a spiral, for which Pessoa provides his own definition:

> ...if we remember that to say is to renew, we will have no trouble defining a spiral: it's a circle that rises without ever closing. I realize that most people would never dare define it this way, for they suppose that defining is to say what others want us to say rather than what's required for the definition. I'll say it more accurately: a spiral is a potential circle that winds round as it rises, without ever completing itself. But no, the definition is still abstract. I'll resort to the concrete, and all will become clear: a spiral is a snake without a snake, vertically wound around nothing[19].

---

[18] P. Silva McNeill. Sacred Geometry of Being: Pessoa's Esoteric Imagery and the Geometry of Modernism

[19] Pessoa. Book of Disquite, 117. Translated by R.Zenith

Pessoa in his ponderings about the «circle winding around nothing» was probably debating with famous Pascal statement about «a sphere, which has its center everywhere and its circumference nowhere». Pessoa's thoughts in that regard a similar with the observations made by Rene Guenon on center and circumference in his work «Symbolism of the cross». There Guenon similarly concludes that it is circumference, as representation of space, that is precisely everywhere, while the center, as the principle of circumference, is nowhere, since the point is defined as the absence of any spatial dimension. Or, as Pessoa put it: «The point, as a negation of space, represents its life».

Pessoa then talks about the fact the spiral is wound vertically, meaning it is just one turn of the helix. In «Symbolism of the cross», Guenon extensively talks about the symbolism of spiral and helix. Spiral represents one state of the being, for example, a human state. Yet the ends of the spiral do not belong to the plane of the spiral, but to adjacent planes, and thus correspond to the points of entry into human state, birth and death, which, as such, are the only two events that are outside of human control.

A circle winding around nothing (its center) is then a symbol of nothing, of the abyss. Another metaphor of the abyss is a Well, as Pessoa says:

> We never know self-realization. We are two abysses — a well staring at the sky[20].

As Bernardo Soares says: «Stepping back from myself, I see that I'm the bottom of a well». Pessoa clearly states that visible world, where we live, is symbol and shadow, while life that we know with our senses is death and sleep. The goal of initiation is to realize that there is no sleep and no death under the «cypress tree».

---

[20] Pessoa. Book of Disquite, 11. Translated by R.Zenith.

THREEFOLD PATH

But first it must be mentioned that Pessoa considered the initiation path to be threefold. In fact he writes about the importance of such triple structure in the «Way of Serpent»:

> Everything is triple, but the triple being of each thing consists in three grades or layers — one low, another medium, another high. Everything which takes place in a layer is reflected and features in another. This is the fundamental principle of all secret science, and it was thus represented by Hermes Trismegistos in the formulation «that which is above is the same as below, and that which is below is as that which is above[21].

In the letter to Adolfo Casais Monteiro on January 13, 1935 Pessoa revealed these three ways as magic, mysticism and alchemy:

> There are three ways to the occult: the magical path (including practices such as spiritism, intellectually the level of witchcraft, which is magic too), this extremely dangerous in every way; the mystical path, which has no properly dangers, but it is uncertain and slow; and what is called the alchemical path, the most difficult and most perfect of all because it involves a transmutation of one's own personality that

21 Pessoa. Way of Serpent

> prepares her, without great risks, rather with defenses than others paths do not have[22].

The preparation for initiation was outlined in an essay «On Initiation». According to Pessoa there are four temptations of the World, that need to be transcended — science (concrete intelligence), philosophy (abstract intelligence), dogma, and critical Intelligence:

> Dogma that ties him to others. Science that ties him to Nature. Philosophy that ties him to the mind of others. His own Philosophy that ties him to himself. The World is all of that. Once he will have crossed these four stages of the first level- that of the Neophyte, he is ready for initiation[23].

The starting point is the scientific discoveries and the philosophical systems, through studying which and cross examination one transitions from concrete intelligence to abstract intelligence. Next, there has to be detachment from the religious dogmas of the Church and indoctrination of customs and traditions. Deeper acquaintance with other religious systems is also necessary. Science is the study of nature of others, philosophy is the study of the mind of others and dogma is study of the spirit of others.

---

[22] R. Zenith. The Selected Prose of Fernando Pessoa

[23] Pessoa. On initiation

Yet, after that one must create his own «system of interpretation of the universe as consistent as possible on the three planes of truth, beauty and ethics». Next step is to abandon his own system in order to become a Neophyte. Science, philosophy, dogma and self constitute the World that must be overcome.

At this point the initiate chooses one of the paths — mystical, magical or gnostic. After, finishing one path, he selects the next one and then the last one. These are three stages that overcome three temptations of the Flesh in order to become and Adept. The desires are quenched by mysticism, the procrastinations are overpowered by magic and the lures are defeated by gnosis. After that Adept obtains the union of knowledge and life. At the level of the Master «one must then strive to the occurring occasion to destroy that achieved unity for the benefit of an even higher one, in a transcendent lucid dynamic realization that baffles our very own understanding».

Above description of the initiatic path pretty much outlines Pessoa's life as summarized by Bernardo Soares in the «Book of Disquiet»:

> After studying metaphysics and sciences, I went on to mental occupations that were more threatening to my nervous equilibrium. I spent

> frightful nights hunched over tomes by mystics and cabbalists which I never had the patience to read except intermittently, trembling and... The rites and mysteries of the Rosicrucians, the symbolism of the Cabbala and the Templars ... — all of this oppressed me for a long time. My feverish days were filled with pernicious speculations based on the demonic logic of metaphysics — magic, alchemy — and I derived a false vital stimulus from the painful and quasi-psychic sensation of being always on the verge of discovering a supreme mystery. I lost myself in the delirious subsystems of metaphysics, systems full of disturbing analogies and pitfalls for lucid thought, vast enigmatic landscapes where glimmers of the supernatural arouse mysteries on the fringes[24].

Pessoa deciphers the next stages of the path in the essay «On Initiation»

> The first temptation to overcome to avoid the errors met alongside the **path** is the World. The second temptation to overcome to avoid the errors met alongside the **Inn** is the Flesh. The third temptation to overcome to avoid the errors of the **Crypt** is the Devil. Temptations are common to all paths, but the mystics are more exposed to the temptation of the World, the magicians to the temptation of the Flesh and the gnostics to the temptation of the Devil[25].

---

[24] Pessoa. Book of Disquite, 251. Translated by R.Zenith.

We, thus, see the following order: first go errors of the path (Highway), which represent World (temptation of mystics), second error is the Inn of Flesh (temptation of magicians), third errors of the Crypt (Devil, temptation of gnostics). Then, in an essay on «How someone in search for Initiation must prepare?» Pessoa confirms the same order with specific focus on temptations of the Flesh, unfolding them into desires, procrastinations and lures:

> He will have to overcome the three temptations that rule the Flesh — the desires that are quenched by **mysticism**, the procrastinations that are overpowered by **magic** and the lures that are defeated by **gnosis**. He must prevail. The Adept during these three stages progress towards the union of knowledge and life[26].

Mysticism goes before magic. Besides different texts, Pessoa left multiple schematic drawings of initiation steps. In those drawing, like famous Pyramid (BNP/E3, 53—96), mysticism is lower than magic. We will follow this logic in the book and the reasons for that will be explained later.

It has to be noted that Pessoa contradicts himself in this matter quite a lot, often putting magic

---

[25] Pessoa. On initiation

[26] Pessoa. How to prepare for initiation

before mysticism. In his famous poem «Initiation» Pessoa starts from the Inn, then goes through Highway (path) to end in the Cave (Crypt):

You aren't asleep under the cypress trees,
For in this world there is no sleep.
Your body is the shadow of the clothes
That conceal your deeper self.
When night, which is death, arrives,
The shadow ends without having been.
And you go, unaware, into that night
As the mere outline of yourself.
But at the **Inn of Wonderment**,
The Angels take away your cape;
You continue with no cape on your shoulders
And little else to cover you.
Then the **Highway** Archangels
Strip you and leave you naked,
Without any clothes, with nothing:
You have just your body, which is you.
Finally, deep within the **cave**,
The Gods strip you even more.
Your body, or outer soul, ceases,
But you see that they are your equals.
The shadow of your clothes remains
Among us in the realm of Destiny.
You are not dead amid **cypress trees**.
Neophyte, there is no death[27]

We can see that the deeper self, which is the true reality, is immersed in this world, which is

---

[27] R.Zenith. A Little Larger Than the Entire Universe

actually an illusion, which consists of three covers: body, clothes and shadow (cape).

Your body is the shadow of the clothes
That conceal your deeper self.

These illusions have to be overcome during initiation, which, correspondingly, consists of three stages along the threefold path. One starts at the Inn of Wonderment, which corresponds to the flesh or cape. The procrastinations are conquered by might of magic with the help of Angels, thus taking away the cape.

But at the Inn of Wonderment,
The Angels take away your cape;
You continue with no cape on your shoulders
And little else to cover you.

Next, one takes the path (Highway), where with the help of Archangels sheds the World or clothes with the help of mysticism, overcoming desires by actually walking the path:

Then the **Highway** Archangels
Strip you and leave you naked,
Without any clothes, with nothing:
You have just your body, which is you.

Finally, in the cave (Crypt) with the help of Gods adept conquers lures of devil and sheds the body. This is done by practicing gnosis or alchemy:

Finally, deep within the **cave**,

The Gods strip you even more.
Your body, or outer soul, ceases,
But you see that they are your equals.

From the cave adept ascends to the top of the tower or castle, which in this poem is represented by the cypress tree. In general, perhaps the stages of this path Pessoa was able to observe in real life at the Initiation Well in Sintra.

Pessoa explains more the difference between them in essay «On Initiation»:

> The paths of mysticism and magic are paths where trickery and errors are often encountered. **Mysticism** implies to mainly trust intuition; magic implies essentially to rely on might. Intuition is a work of the mind that allows us to access the results of the working intelligence without using it. Might, in the sense of magical power, is a work of the mind that allows to benefit from the results of continuous effort without indulging in it. Mysticism and magic, even if they need time to work, are shortcuts towards knowledge. ... Mysticism seeks to transcend the intellect (with intuition), magic seeks to transcend the intellect by might (power); gnosis seeks to transcend the intellect with a higher intellect.[28]

---

[28] Pessoa. On initiation

Magic, according to Pessoa's other classification is external or symbolic initiation, which strengthens the will and goes through phases of life but not comprehension. Mysticism is outer internal or intellectual initiation, that strengthens intellect and candidate goes through stages of comprehension but not life. Alchemy is an internal or vital initiation, where candidate «lives what he fills and knows». After three stages initiate reaches the «union of knowledge and life».

«Union of knowledge and life» means union between the Biblical Tree of Life and Tree of knowledge of good and evil. Interestingly, both trees were in the center of paradise, one of which was surrounded by serpent. Pessoa writes about the serpent:

> The Serpent is the understanding of all things and the intellectual comprehension of the emptiness of them (...) The understanding of everything, the fusion of the opposites, the science of the indifference of good and evil, the science of the value of emotion as emotion and the will as will, the equal irony to the wise as to the naive[29].

Thus, the snake unites the opposites of Tree of knowledge of good and evil and brings straight

---

[29] Esp. 54A-2

to the Tree of Life, the Consciousness:

> Consciousness transcends unity. It is the absolute point that «exists» only: in fact, for something to exist, it must exist infinitely in it. The point, as a negation of space, represents its life.

The point, that exists, is God. Pessoa continues in the «Way of the Serpent»:

> To exist, in the true sense of the word, means to be God, that is, to have created oneself; in other words, do not depend substantially on anything or anyone... Magic and alchemy are illusory paths. The truth lies only in the direct instinct (symbolically represented by the horns) and in the straight line of its ascension to the supreme instinct — in the direct instinct, whose active form is sexuality, whose intermediate form is imagination, fantasy, or creation in the spirit, whose final form is the creation of God, union with God, abstract and absolute identification with oneself, truth[30].

Going Back to Pessoa's understanding of magic as life without comprehension, mysticism as comprehension without life and alchemy as the «living knowledge», we can see that the way of the serpent means not embracing them all, but passing through them to the peak, or the point, which is God. From that peak, all the paths

---

30 Pessoa. Way of serpent

become illusory and have to be rejected. We must live through something, in order to have the right to transcend it:

> It costs nothing, to those who are unable to feel Christianity, to repudiate it; it costs everything to repudiate it after having really felt it, after having lived it, after being it. What it costs is to repudiate it, or to know how to repudiate it, not as a form of lie, but as a form of truth. Recognize truth as truth, and at the same time as error; live the opposites without accepting them; to feel everything in all ways, and not to be anything else, in the end, if not the understanding of everything — when man rises to this peak, he is free, as on every peak, he is alone, as on every peak, he is united to heaven, to which he is never united, as on every peak[31].

Why does Christianity, as a set of dogmas and concepts, have to be repudiated? Because as an expression of illusory ego, it has the reality only within the sphere of ego, but after realization of God its concepts become as illusory as the ego.

Later Pessoa was envisioning the reconciliation of life (or faith) and reason as his political goal. He wrote to his aunt Anica that:

> In the V spiritual Empire there will be a meeting of the two separate forces ...: The left

---

[31] Nuno Ribeiro. Pessoa Philosophical Essays: A Critical Edition

> side of knowledge — science, reason; and the right side of intuition — mysticism, spirituality...[32]

The Fifth Spiritual Empire was supposed to be the new «Spiritual India»:

> And our Race will leave in search of a new India, which does not exist in space because it is made of dreams... in which the discoveries of the Portuguese navigators were the obscure and carnal anti-thrust... and the true and supreme destiny ...will be fulfilled divinely.

[32] Paulo Martins. The Influence of Indian Philosophy and Spirituality in the Work of Fernando Pessoa: Some Perspectives

FOUR HETERONYMS

The goal of all Esoterism is to achieve union with God after achieving union of knowledge and life. The latter corresponds to realization of the state of «perfect man», as explained by Rene Guenon in his work «Great Triad», while the former is about becoming «transcendent man».

Pessoa has a whole passage summarizing his thought on what the union with God is intended to mean:

> Union with God means therefore the repetition by the Adept of the Divine Act of Creation, by which he is identical with God in act, or manner of act, but, at the same time, an inversion of the Divine Act, by which he is still divided from God, or God's opposite, else he were God Himself and no union were required[33].

This creation consisted in «the conversion by God of His own consciousness into the plural consciousness of separate being». «Be plural like the universe!» exclaims Pessoa. The creation of multiple Pessoa heteronyms is thus an act of imitating God and an attempt of achieving union with God. In «Time's passage» Campos writes:

> I multiplied myself to feel myself,

---

[33] Pessoa. On initiation

> To feel myself I had to feel everything,
> I overflowed, I did nothing but spill out, I undressed, I yielded,
> And in each corner of my soul there's an altar to a different god.

Similarly, Bernardo Soares describes:

> To create in myself a nation with its own politics, parties and revolutions, and to be all of it, everything, to be God in the real pantheism of this people-I, to be the substance and movement of their bodies and their souls, of the very ground they tread and the acts they perform! To be everything, to be them and not them! Ah, this is one of the dreams I'm still far from realizing. And if I realized it, perhaps I would die. I'm not sure why, but it seems one couldn't live after committing such a great sacrilege against God, after usurping the divine power of being everything[34].

Creation of heteronyms was the «greatest act of intellectual magic» of his imagination. This creation process is identical to the one in the dream state, with the only difference that it is implemented in the physical reality. The imaginary creation allows for creation of multiple personalities, while at the same being one. It is obvious that in the dream, although one clearly identifies oneself as a specific entity, the

---

[34] Pessoa. Book of Disquite, 157. Translated by R.Zenith.

other people, that are present in that dream, are created and simultaneously played by the same modality. This is clearly described by none other than Rene Guenon in his book «Multiple states of being»:

> Naturally all these other roles appear secondary to the one that is principal to the individual, that is, the one in which his current consciousness is directly involved, and since all the elements of the dream exist only through this individual, one can say that they are real only insofar as they participate in his own existence; it is the dreamer himself who realizes them as so many modifications of himself, without ceasing thereby to be himself independently of these modifications, which in no way affect what constitutes the very essence of his individuality. Moreover, if the individual is conscious that he is dreaming, conscious, that is, of the fact that all the events unfolding in this state have only the reality that he himself gives them, he will be entirely unaffected even if in the dream he is simultaneously actor and spectator, and this is so precisely because he will not cease to be a spectator in order to become an actor, the conception and the realization no longer being separated for his individual consciousness when it has reached a stage of development sufficient to embrace synthetically all the present modifications of the individuality. If the situation is otherwise, the same modifications can still be realized, but if the

> consciousness does not link this realization directly to the conception of which it is an effect, the individual is led to attribute to the dream events a reality exterior to himself, and, in the measure in which he does so, he is subject to an illusion of which the cause lies within himself, an illusion consisting in separating the multiplicity of those events from their immediate principle, that is to say from his own individual unity. This is a **very clear example of a multiplicity existing within a unity, without the latter being affected by it**; and even though the unity in question here may only be relative-that of an individual in relation to that multiplicity, it nonetheless plays a part analogous to that of veritable and primordial unity in relation to universal manifestation[35].

The process, which many people realize in dreams, Pessoa projected into material reality. For him, the border between material and imaginary disappeared. Usually people think that the material reality is real, while the imaginary is not real. For Pessoa it is the other way around:

> Only what we dream is what we truly are, because all the rest, having been realized, belongs to the world and to everyone.
>
> My imaginary world has always been the only true world for me. I've never had loves so real and so full of verve and blood and life as the

[35] Rene Guenon. Multiple states of being.

> ones I've had with characters I myself created. What madness! I miss them because, like all loves, these kind also come and go...[36]

The imagined heteronyms are, thus, more real, than actual people:

> There are metaphors more real than the people who walk in the street. There are images tucked away in books that live more vividly than many men and women. There are phrases from literary works that have a positively human personality[37].

Bernardo Soares heteronym confides:

> I've never done anything but dream. This, and this alone, has been the meaning of my life. My only real concern has been my inner life... The only thing I've loved is nothing at all...[38]

In a preliminary draft of the letter on the heteronyms to Adolfo Casais Monteiro, Pessoa, in the last year of his life, reflects on the origin of the heteronyms in his childhood games:

> This may seem merely like a child's imagination that gives life to dolls. But it was more than that. I intensely conceived those characters with no need of dolls. Distinctly visible in my ongoing dream, they were utterly

---

[36] Pessoa. Book of Disquite, 348. Translated by R.Zenith.

[37] Ibid 157

[38] Ibid 92

> human realities for me, which any doll — because unreal — would have spoiled. They were people[39].

In the final draft of the letter to Casais Monteiro on the genesis of the heteronyms, Pessoa begins the description of his childhood friends thus:

> Ever since I was a child, it has been my tendency to create around me a fictitious world, to surround myself with friends and acquaintances that never existed. (I can't be sure, of course, if they really never existed, or if it's me who doesn't exist. In this matter, as in any other, we shouldn't be dogmatic[40].

After tracing the development of his «spontaneous tendency to depersonalization' through his adolescence and early adulthood, Pessoa writes:

> Today, I have no personality: I've divided all my humanness among the various authors whom I've served as literary executor. Today I'm the meeting-place of a small humanity that belongs only to me. This is simply the result of a dramatic temperament taken to the extreme. My dramas, instead of being divided into acts full of action, are divided into souls. That's what this apparently baffling phenomenon comes down to. I don't reject — in fact, I'm all

---

39 R. Zenith, Pessoa: A Biography

40 R. Zenith. The Selected Prose of Fernando Pessoa

> for — psychiatric explanations, but it should be understood that all higher mental activity, because it's abnormal, is equally subject to psychiatric interpretation. I don't mind admitting that I'm crazy, but I want it to be understood that my craziness is no different from Shakespeare's, whatever may be the comparative value of the products that issue from the saner side of our crazed minds[41].

The initiation path, as mentioned before, is threefold, consisting of magic, mysticism and alchemy, and in his poetry Pessoa mastered all three ways. With respect to magic he writes, that the creation of heteronyms was an act of intellectual magic:

> The creation of Caeiro and of the discipleship of Reis and Campos seems, at first sight, an elaborate joke of the imagination. But it is not. It [is] **a great act of intellectual magic**, a magnum opus of the impersonal creative power.
>
> I need all the concentration I can have for the preparation of what may be called, figuratively as an act of intellectual magic — that is to say, for the preparation of a literary creation in a, so to speak, fourth dimension of the mind[42].

As Pessoa explains further, mysticism is higher

---

[41] R. Zenith, Pessoa: A Biography

[42] R. Zenith. The Selected Prose of Fernando Pessoa

than magic. This is another time, where Pessoa changes order of magic and mysticism:

> The mystic has, in his scale of initiation, a higher place than the magician. Someone like the Count of Saint-Germain, or Cagliostro, supposing they are what we were told they are, are less initiated then a S. Francis of Assis or a Saint Therese of Jesus. Magic is the highest point of low initiation; mysticism the lowest of high initiation. Magic is the highest grade of the force of man as a man; mysticism is the lowest grade of force of man as an angel, this is, /united/ to God. /Above this only what is one with God, the occultist/[43].

Obviously, poetry is a form of mysticism:

> Mysticism abides in literature, in poetic literature especially.
>
> This depends on the nature of poetry. Poetry is essentially mystical. Its essence is an abnormality by deficiency of critical and excess of emotional activity, contained, withheld by its own laws, and by no other laws.
>
> Mysticism, in its turn, involves poetry, it is a species of poetry — itself, though really the essence of it.
>
> A [lexander] S [earch][44]

---

[43] P. Ellen Bothe. Notes on Mysticism and Poetry in Fernando Pessoa

[44] Ibid

According to Pessoa, mystic deals with symbols of reality rather than with reality itself, which is the domain of magic:

> But let us understand each other well. I call a poet mystic if he is a poet of ideas who gives the things we call real a merely symbolic value and finds among them occult and intimate relations of a different order as those that science recognizes. I do not use «mysticism' /here/ in its psychological sense, in the sense in which Nordau used the word[45].

As his heteronym Alexander Search poetically expressed it in the poem «The Circle»:

> My simpler thoughts in vain had stemmed
> The current of this madness free,
> But that my thinking is condemned
> To **symbol** and **analogy**

The alchemical path, according to Pessoa, involves transmutation of ones own personality, and that was precisely the creation of the heteronyms. As he explains this transmutation himself in the same letter:

> Once Alberto Caeiro had appeared, I instinctively and subconsciously tried to find disciples for him. From Caeiro's false paganism I extracted the latent Ricardo Reis, at last discovering his name and adjusting him to his true self, for now I actually saw him. And

---

[45] Ibid

then a new individual, quite the opposite of Ricardo Reis, suddenly and impetuously came to me. In an unbroken stream, without interruptions or corrections, the ode whose name is «Triumphal Ode», by the man whose name is none other than Бlvaro de Campos, issued from my typewriter.

And so I created a nonexistent coterie, placing it all in a framework of reality. I ascertained the influences at work and the friendships between them, I listened in myself to their discussions and divergent points of view, and in all of this it seem**s that I, who created them all, was the one who was least there**. It seems that it all went on without me. And thus it seems to go on still. If one day I'm able to publish the aesthetic debate between Ricardo Reis and Alvaro de Campos, you'll see how different they are, and how I have nothing to do with the matter[46].

In the essay «On Initiation» Pessoa actually suggests that poetry is the end of initiation and its three stages — neophyte, adept and master — have corresponding levels in poetry:

Let us suppose that the writing of great poetry is the end of initiation. The Neophyte stage will be the acquisition of the cultural elements which the poet will have to deal with when writing poetry — being, grade by grade and in

---

[46] R. Zenith. The Selected Prose of Fernando Pessoa

> what seems to me to be an exact analogy: (0) grammar, (1) general culture, (2) particular literary culture, (3) [... Blank space in original document] The adept stage will be, drawing out the analogy in the same manner: (5) the writing of simple lyrical poetry, as in common lyric, (6) the writing of complex lyrical poetry, as in [... Blank space in original document] (7) the writing of ordered or philosophical lyrical poetry, as in the ode. The master stage will be, in the same manner: (8) the writing of epic poetry, (9) the writing of dramatic poetry, (10) the fusing of all poetry, lyric, epic and dramatic, into something beyond all these[47].

It can be said that Pessoa himself have written a number of Odes, like «Maritime Ode» corresponding to step seven. His Mensagem is an example of epic poetry of step eight. In the end, his heteronyms are the fusion of step ten.

Despite multiplying himself into over seventy distinct personalities, there were only three main heteronyms, which Pessoa esplores most of the time. In the Letter to Adolfo Casais Monteiro Pessoa describes the dynamic among them.

> How do I write in the name of these three? Caeiro, through sheer and unexpected inspiration, without knowing or even suspecting that I'm going to write in his name.

[47] Pessoa. On Initiation.

> Ricardo Reis, after an abstract meditation, which suddenly takes concrete shape in an ode. Campos, when I feel a sudden impulse to write and don't know what. (My semi-heteronym Bernardo Soares, who in many ways resembles Alvaro de Campos, always appears when I'm sleepy or drowsy, so that my qualities of inhibition and rational thought are suspended; his prose is an endless reverie. He's a semi-heteronym because his personality, although not my own, doesn't differ from my own but is a mere mutilation of it. He's me without my rationalism and emotions. His prose is the same as mine, except for certain formal restraint that reason imposes on my own writing, and his Portuguese is exactly the same — whereas Caeiro writes bad Portuguese, Campos writes it reasonably well but with mistakes such as «me myself» instead of «I myself», etc.., and Reis writes better than I, but with a purism I find excessive.[48]

Including Pessoa himself and his semi-heteronym, alter ego, Bernardo Soares, that gives us five major heteronyms. Next, we will try to show how these major heteronyms correspond to the degrees of Initiation. Stage of neophyte, which is technically outside of initiation, clearly corresponds to Baron of Teive,

[48] Pessoa. Book of Disquite. Translated by R.Zenith

who was studying philosophy and science, and considered himself a Stoic. It will be shown later why Ricardo Reis is clearly a mystic. Pessoa himself, as the creator of sensationism, is a magician. Pessoa was unclear on what is higher, magic or mysticism. Here, based on our later comments on Yoga, we will show why magic must be higher than mysticism. Alberto Caeiro was unequivocally a Master. Which leaves Alvaro de Campos and Bernardo Soares, as alchemists, like two sides of the same coin. Each of the heteronyms can be characterized by one quote, that is most representative, in our opinion, of their poetic essence and which also corresponds to the stages of progression in nondual awareness, which will be explained in the next section of the book.

NEOPHYTE BARON OF TEIVE: «WHERE INTELLIGENCE EXISTS, LIFE IS IMPOSSIBLE»

Baron of Teive had self, so he had to commit suicide. His self was immersed in duality, split between moral and intellectual sentiment, which he recognized himself in the «Education of Stoic», his only manuscript:

> For a man to be utterly and absolutely moral, he has to be a bit stupid. For a man to be absolutely intellectual, he has to be a bit immoral. I don't know what game or irony of creation makes it impossible for man to be both things at once. And yet, to my misfortune, this duality occurs in me[49].

This duality generates a conflict «between emotional need for faith and the intellectual impossibility of believing», between «futility of all effort and vanity of all plans».

Based on the title of his only manuscript and the fact that he was practicing detachment, it can be

---

[49] Pessoa. The Education of the Stoic: The Only Manuscript of the Baron of Teive. Translated by R.Zenith

concluded, that Baron considered himself a Stoic. Yet, the goal of stoicism was about achieving happiness in life through aligning with four cardinal virtues, and in that regard Baron miserably failed. These four virtues are prudence, justice, courage and temperance. The goal of stoic life was to seek prudence and live according to it for the sake of his spirit, act with justice and kindness for the sake of others, master his desires for the sake of the body, and practice these three virtues with courage. Stoics devised their curriculum into three sciences: Logic, Ethics, and Physics. Logic was concerned with spirit, intellect and prudence, ethics was concerned with justice and action towards others, while physics was concerned with the body and material world, temperance towards the body and courage to overcome the elements.

Justice is the he unanimity of the soul with itself, the state of obedience to moral laws, yet most of the Baron's thought were about seducing girls. Temperance is self-control, from things like overeating, overthinking and overindulging, yet Baron admits his constant overthinking, which results in lack of action. Prudence according to Stoic definitions is the knowledge of what is good and bad, the knowledge that produces happiness. Baron writes that he «had all the conditions for happiness, save happiness». «Modern man, if he is unhappy, is a pessimist», notes Baron and pessimism, in its turn, «is a result of sexual rejection».

But, the most lacking virtue in Baron was the courage, which is the state of the soul unmoved by fear, and it comes down to Baron's indecision and inability to act. Comparing his life to the battle, Baron observes that «cowardice did not even make it to the battlefield»:

> He didn't dare implement his battle plan, since it was sure to be imperfect, and he didn't dare perfect it, since his conviction that it would never be perfect, killed all his desire to strife for perfection.[50]

«We value what we think rather than what we do», says Baron, «forgetting that the first function of life is action». He was not acting, because things felt banal, but when he saw other people doing them, he realized they were normal. «Scruples are the death of action».

By missing out on phenomenon of life, he was also missing out on love. More specifically he was talking about women in a chapter with the telling name «Why the Baron did not seduce

---

[50] Ibid

more girls». His intellect always found flaws in women, one was too big, too small, too delicate, unattractive. In the end:

> The girls I didn't seduce were seduced by others, for it was inevitable that somebody seduce them. I had scruples where other men didn't think twice, and after seeing what I didn't do, done by others, I wondered: Why did I think so much if it only made me suffer?[51]

He even had a chance, as he explained, to marry a simple girl, «but between me and her, in my soul's indecision, stood fourteen generations of barons and a mental image of the whole town smirking at my wedding»:

> And, so I, the man of reason and detachment, lost out on happiness, because of the neighbors I disdain[52].

Thus, mental image, which is an outcome of heredity and upbringing, and is not real, none the less becomes the obstacle for love in real life. This mental image is the cause of unhappiness not only for Baron, but for the whole humanity. As Baron puts it, «we create in ourselves an interpretation» of the world, the world that we cannot really know, but we are using this interpretation as the measure of all things. Using

---

[51] Ibid

[52] Ibid

modern analogy, if the reality is the territory, then our interpretation of this reality is a map, and it is clear that map is not the territory:

> My whole life has been a battle lost on the map[53].

Baron confesses that he wasted his life on the map without even showing up to the actual battlefield. This «interpretation in ourselves», formed by our heredity and education, is basically what constitutes our idea of ourselves, our ego. And, because in reality this interpretation is only a map and not the real territory, it is in essence a hallucination. Thus, the whole notion of self as such is a hallucination:

> It's a hallucination in the strict sense, being an illusion based on something only dimly seen[54].

His own interpretation of his self, which is expressed in the manuscript «Education of stoics», Baron asks to take it not as a confession, but as a «definition» of himself. In a way, all Pessoa heteronyms are just such different definitions or narratives. Contemporary psychologist Jerome Bruner argues that our «life is a narrative». We only live in a present

---

53 Ibid

54 Ibid

moment, which always escapes us. So humans organize their experiences and memories in the form of myths, narrative stories, excuses, which do not even have to be logical or empirically verifiable. Bruner writes:

> Narratives, then, are a version of reality whose acceptability is governed by convention and «narrative necessity» rather than by empirical verification and logical requiredness[55].

Baron also notices the schism between the narrative and life in all religious people, which «think like spiritualists and act like materialists»:

> What's the life of humanity but a religious evolution with no influence on daily life?[56]

Hence, comes a similar conclusion of Bernardo Soares in the «Book of disquiet», that «Christ is a form of emotion».

With respect to Pessoa's steps of initiation, it is obvious, that Baron can be positioned at the stage of Neophyte, where he was supposed to study all the scientific and philosophical systems, create his own and then reject it. Baron writes:

---

55 J Bruner. The Narrative Construction of Reality

56 Pessoa. The Education of the Stoic: The Only Manuscript of the Baron of Teive. Translated by R.Zenith

> I began by elaborating a kind of psychological epistemology. To help me understand systems, I created a method for analyzing those who produce them[57].

As a result, he discovered that «philosophy is no more than expression of temperament», similarly to the observation, that Christ is a form of emotion. After realizing that, he came to «radical renunciation of all metaphysical speculation»:

> I feel that I have attained the full use of my reason. And that's why I am going to kill myself[58].

We return to the point where we started. «Full use of reason» means remaining in duality of reason, in constant mental conversation within one's self, in «hallucination», which does not exist. But, in order to enjoy life through the senses, which only exists in present infinitesimal moment, one must stop the mental dialogue, stop thinking and just be in the present moment of what is. Hence, Baron says, that where intelligence exists, life is impossible:

> It is impossible to live life according to reason. Intelligence provides no guiding rule. This realization unveiled for me what is perhaps

---

57 Ibid

58 Ibid

> hidden in the myth of the Fall. As when one's physical gaze is struck by lightning, my soul's vision was struck by the terrible and true meaning of the temptation that led Adam to eat from the so-called Tree of Knowledge. **Where intelligence exists, life is impossible**[59].

Cessation of mental dialogue results in the death of ego. This realization is the beginning of the path of nondual awareness. At the end of this path we come to Caeiro's: «I have no philosophy, I have senses».

---

[59] Ibid

MYSTIC RICARDO REIS: «I LET LIFE PASS ME BY»

If Baron of Teive was a stoic, Ricardo Reis «was a stoic without harshness of stoicism», according to Reis himself. This makes him more of an Epicurean, rather than stoic. Pessoa himself called Reis «Greek Horace», as he was also known for his odes. But Horace is not just the poet according to Bernardo Soares:

> Horace said that the just man will remain undaunted, even if the world crumbles all around him. Although the image is absurd, the point is valid. Even if what we pretend to be (because we coexist with others) crumbles around us, we should remain undaunted — not because we're just, but because we're ourselves, and to be ourselves means having nothing to do with external things that crumble, even if they crumble right on top of what for them we are[60].

Because we are what we are, that is ourselves and not external things, we should remain detached from them and remain undaunted, even when the external world around us crumbling. Reis as the incarnation of Horace, described this state in his «Chess Players»:

> Houses were burning, walls were torn down

[60] Pessoa. Book of Disquite, 162. Translated by R.Zenith.

> And coffers plundered;
> Women were raped and propped against
> The crumbling walls;
> Children, pierced by spears, were so much
> Blood in the streets...
> But the two chess players stayed where they were,
> Close to the city
> And far from its clamor, and kept on playing
> Their game of chess[61].

The world was crumbling, «women were raped» and «children pierced by spears», but they were «playing their game of chess». The initial response of the human being in such situation would be flight or fight. Yet, the mastery of the will is such that they do no nothing and continue to play chess. Bernardo Soares again explains it in the following way:

> All of life's unpleasant experiences — when we make fools of ourselves, act thoughtlessly, or lapse in our observance of some virtue — should be regarded as mere external accidents which can't affect the substance of our soul. We should see them as toothaches or calluses of life, as things that bother us but remain outside us (even though they're ours), or that only our organic existence need consider and our vital functions worry about.

---

61 R.Zenith. A Little Larger Than the Entire Universe

> When we achieve this attitude, which in essence is that of the mystics, we're protected not only from the world but also from ourselves, for we've conquered what is foreign in us, contrary and external to us, and therefore our enemy[62].

Here we clearly see that Pessoa classifies Reis as a mystic, since he has an attitude of the mystic. In «Philosophical essay» Pessoa says that will does not exist on its own, but within a sphere of feeling. And mystic is the one, who transcended the errors of the feelings. Another Reis poem reflects this mystical attitude:

> I prefer roses, my love, to my country
> And I love magnolias more than I do
> Glory and virtue
>
> So long as life does not tire me out.
> **I let life pass me by** life pass me by
> While I remain unchanged
>
> What can it matter to the one to whom
> Nothing any longer matters that one wins
> And another loses, so long as the dawn breaks
>
> If each year in the Spring
> Leaves show forth
> That in the Fall cease to be?

---

[62] Pessoa. Book of Disquite, 162. Translated by R.Zenith.

As for the rest of it, those other things human beings
Attach to life,
What increase can they bring to my soul?

Nothing — save a desire for indifference
And the certain indolence
Of the fugitive hour.[63]

Reis prefers roses to country and magnolias to virtues, because they exist in the present moment, while country and virtue and glory are simply ideas of the mind. So, he «lets life pass him by while he remains unchanged».

As long as I have the full breeze in my hair
And see the sun shinning bright on the leaves
I will not ask for more.
What better thing can destiny give me
Than the **sensual passing of time in moments**
Of ignorance like this?
Wise is the one who does not seek
The seeker will find in all things
The abyss, and doubt in himself[64]

Yet, with passing time we also pass like a river. Reis writes in «Lydia»:

Then let us think, as grown up children, that life

---

[63] G. Monteiro. Twenty-two New Translations: English renditions of Pessoa's heteronymous Portuguese poems

[64] R.Zenith. Fernando Pessoa & Co. : selected poems

Passes and does not stay, nothing stops or ever turns back,
It goes towards a sea very far away, towards where Fate is,
Further away than the gods.
Let us stop holding hands, for it is not worth tiring ourselves.
Whether we enjoy or not, **we pass with the river**.
Better to know how to pass silently
And without great disquiet.

Ricardo Reis, being the first disciple of master Caeiro, approaches the master himself. Not only he let's life pass him by, undaunted by unpleasant experiences, like a mystic, but like a master he enjoys the «sensual passing of time in moments». He says in «I love what I see…»:

I love what I see, because I will cease
One day or another from seeing it

The ability to see is a miracle that we need to enjoy, since it is our eyesight and brain that creates what we see:

In what I looked at, in part have I remained
When one thing I have seen has passed, I pass as well
Without distinguishing the memory
Of what I have seen from what I have been

That is why you have to «Seize the day, because you are the day»:

Some, having their eyes on the past,
Look at what they cannot see; others, eyes
Staring at the past, look at
What cannot be seen.
Why looking so far at what is close —
Our own safety? This is the day,
This is the time, this is the moment, this
Is what we are, and it is all.
Perennial, the time, which endlessly flows,
Acknowledges us as useless. At the same breath
We live, we will die. Seize
The day, for you are it.[65]

This formula is as powerful as Cairo's «I am the size of what i see». Seize the day, because yesterday and tomorrow do not exist:

Tomorrow does not exist
I am merely a being which exists
In the instant which could be the last
Of this man that I pretend to be

Since «Christ is a form of emotion» or a mental configuration, he is Uncertain as such, unlike the Reality, which is certain and which exists:

Allow me the Reality of each instant
And allow me my immediate and tranquil gods
Which do not reside in Uncertain
But in fields and rivers.

---

65 A. Cardiello, B. Ryan, G. Tusa. Fernando Pessoa and Philosophy

The man, who is free in such a way, is equal to the Gods:

Not just those who envy and hate us
Limit and oppress us; those who love us
Limit us no less.
May the Gods grant me, stripped of all
Affections, the cold freedom of the heights
Of nothingness. Wanting little,
A man has everything. Wanting nothing,
He's free. Not having and not desiring,
He's equal, though man, to the Gods[66].

And if he can be equal to the Gods, the next logical question is why can't he be God:

If for every thing there is a god,
Why then is there no god of me?
Why am I myself not it?
It's in me that god comes alive because I feel
I see the outside world clearly —
Things, men, soulless.
[If each thing has its corresponding god,
Why shouldn't I have a god as well?
Why shouldn't it be me?
It's in me that this god moves, for I feel.
I clearly see the outside world —
Things and men with no soul[67].

Reis approaches the stage of alchemist as well:

Nothing comes of nothing. We are nothing.
Briefly in sun, in air, we postpone

---

66 R.Zenith. A Little Larger Than the Entire Universe

67 Ibid

The unbreathable darkness that weighs us down
And humble earth imposes, Delayed corpses that breed. We're stories telling stories, nothing[68].

[68] Honig and Brown. Pessoa: Poems of Fernando

MAGICIAN FERNANDO PESSOA: «NO REALITY BUT SENSATION»

As was previously observed, in order to become a Neophyte one must study all the scientific and philosophical systems created by other men and then create his own system in order to reject it. And Pessoa did just that. He is credited as the author of multiple -isms: paulism, cubism, intersectionism and sensationism. At the root of intersectionism is the idea that every thing is an intersection. As Bernardo Soares puts it:

> The environment is the soul of things. Each thing has its own expression and this expression comes from outside it. Each thing is the intersection of three lines, and these three lines form the thing: a certain quantity of material, the way in which we interpret it, and the environment it's in. This table on which I'm writing is a block of wood, it's the table, and it's a piece of furniture among others in the room. My impression of this table, if I wish to transcribe it, will be composed of the notions that it is made of wood, that I call it a table and attribute certain uses to it, and that it receives, reflects and is transformed by the objects placed on top of it, in whose juxtaposition it has an external soul. And its very color, the fading of that color, its spots and cracks — all came from outside it, and this (more than its wooden essence) is what gives it its soul. And the core of that soul, its being a

table, also came from the outside, which is its personality[69].

Intersectionism is, thus, three dimensional. Pessoa defined sensationism as the «art of the fourth dimension». Like theosophy is outside all religions, yet, according to Pessoa, it is «the fundamental truth that underlies all religious systems alike». Similarly, sensationism underlies all art and aesthetic things. Every sensation in reality is a mix of several sensations, which is the idea behind intersectionism.

In his «Philosophical essays», while analyzing what is realism, skepticism, agnosticism and rationalism, he is talking about two forms of rationalism, lower and higher. In general, rationalism is belief in reason, that the reason «is all that we have, or best we have, to investigate truth». The main difference between two rationalisms is the definition of truth. Lower rationalism believes that reason can reach metaphysical conclusions, and, as a result, everything coming from faith is false, while higher rationalism is actually confined within physics, since only that can be studied by senses, and does not proclaim something as false even if it is outside of physics:

---

[69] Pessoa. Book of Disquite, 58. Translated by R.Zenith

> Higher rationalism, basing on the premise that all knowledge comes from the senses, and that reason is not a sense, cannot admit the possibility of reason more than sifting the data of the senses; and as there are no known senses (unless the mystics are right, which we cannot verify to universal satisfaction) which supply metaphysical data, reason is powerless to arrive at any conclusion as to the fundamentals of being. All faiths, however absurd they may seem, or contradictory, are therefore possible; they cannot be denounced as false; they must simply be let live as probabilities that never can be verified. This leads to tolerance without an effort.[70]

While lower rationalism contradicts faith, the higher does not. Pessoa also explains it in a different passage:

> For this is only a notion of reality. Reality is not only stones and plants, with a moving sprinkling of animals. It is also the dreams, the visions, the mystical experiences, of the substance and passing of mankind. Christ may not be real as reality, but has been real as an ideality. For the realist, who is the rationalist, that is as enough as the stars. The ideal men have loved is as real as the woman men have loved, for the love is the one actual thing[71].

---

[70] Nuno Ribeiro. Pessoa Philosophical Essays: A Critical Edition

[71] Ibid

This rationale perhaps underlies the creation of sensationism. Pessoa proclaims that, «there is nothing, no reality, but sensation». As Bernardo Soares put it in the «Book of Disquite»: «Nature is the offspring of my sensations». Everything is just different aspects of the «sensation cube»:

> Every sensation (of a solid thing) is a solid body bounded by planes, which are inner images (of the nature of dreams — two-dimensioned), bounded themselves by lines (which are ideas, of one dimension only). Sensationism pretends, taking stock of this real reality, to realize in art a decomposition of reality into its psychic geometrical elements[72].

This is a different way of explaining the Indian concept of the four states of the being, which will be explained in detail later. The waking state experienced by senses is three-dimensional, consisting of solids. «Dreams are sensations with only two dimensions. Ideas are sensations with only one dimension. A line is an idea». That is the main concepts behind Pessoa's cubism:

> From an objective standpoint, the Cube of Sensation is composed of:
> Ideas = lines
> Images (internal) = planes
> Images of objects = solids[73]

---

[72] Ibid

Dot is the consciousness or sensation itself. And because dot has no dimensions, it includes in itself as in principle all other dimensions. Line is a sequence of dots, plane is a sequence of lines and cube is a sequence of planes. Pessoa calls dot «atomic consciousness»: «consciousness is the only immaterial thing that exists, not human consciousness, but general conscience, atomic consciousness, I believe». Modern science suggests that sensation rises from the brain, but according to Pessoa in «Philosophical essays»:

> The nervous system, the brain cannot explain sensation, because the brain and the nervous system are themselves things of sensation. The sensation of colours cannot be properly explained by a movement, because both colour and movement are sensations[74].

Consciousness includes space in itself, as the dot is the principle of cube, and because nervous system also occupies space, it is also within our consciousness or sensation, and thus, cannot really explain it. We cannot really know anything outside our sensations, which means that everything we know is our sensations, it does not have a separate reality of its own.

---

[73] Ibid

[74] Ibid

Object does not exist.

The goal of Art in general and of sensationism in particular is to decompose reality from cube to plane to line in order to get to the dot, which means to «increase human self-consciousness». Since dot has no dimensions it is an essence, a fourth dimension, and sensationism is the «art of fourth dimension». Once someone achieves that, he realizes that:

> 1. The only reality is sensation.
> 2. The maximum reality will be attained by feeling everything in every way (in all times).
> 3. For that one needed to be everything and everyone[75].

Pessoa often uses the metaphor of travel to explore the sensation. When you come to a new place seeing something for the first time, there is feeling of novelty, freshness, when we notice things that would have been ignored otherwise as a background. Bernardo Soares in the «Book of Disquite» writes:

> The argonauts said that it wasn't necessary to live, only to sail. We, argonauts of our pathological sensibility, say that it's not necessary to live, only to feel.[76]

---

[75] Ibid

[76] Pessoa. Book of Disquite, 124. Translated by R.Zenith.

Taking nothing seriously and recognizing our sensations as the only reality we have for certain, we take refuge there, exploring them like large unknown countries.[77]

Inch by inch I conquered the inner terrain I was born with. Bit by bit I reclaimed the swamp in which I'd languished. I gave birth to my infinite being, but I had to wrench myself out of me with forceps[78].

Life is what we make of it. Travel is the traveller. What we see isn't what we see but what we are[79].

---

77 Ibid 1

78 Ibid 15

79 Ibid 451

ALCHEMIST ALVARO DE CAMPOS: «I AM NOTHING»

One of Pessoa's heteronyms, Charles Robert Anon, have attempted to write an «Essay on free will», where he comes to conclusion that the origin of error of free will stems from «synthetic nature of consciousness, making one of many yet not properly a whole». Most of that essay is the elaboration of this thesis. To prove that, Anon in Socratic way poses the main question if the human soul is simple or composed from many parts? And, he proposes a series of arguments to show that: «If the soul is simple, free will is unthinkable. If the soul should be composed free will is impossible».

The statement that the human soul is simple is rejected based on the following logic:

> The human soul is declared to be simple. If it be simple, then all human faculties have the same nature. If all human faculties have the same nature, the intellectual faculties have the same nature as, for instance, the appetitive or regulative faculties[80].

This logically implies, that if the soul is simple, the soul that thinks is the same as the soul that

---

[80] Nuno Ribeiro. Pessoa Philosophical Essays: A Critical Edition

tastes food, and that if one can make himself good or evil, he can easily make himself idiot or genius, which is false or impossible. This makes the first premise false and implies that the soul might be composite, and that there are many ways how it could possibly be. It can be composite based on position (part of should be in the head, part in the gut), the different parts can have different nature, or soul parts can differ from each other in degree. Anon writes:

> The Human soul is either simple or composed: that is to say, either it is the whole and the same soul which thinks, feels, desires, calculates, perceives; or each faculty or manifestation of the soul or the soul is made up of several faculties separate and distinct from one another, which have each its own function, and nothing to do with the function of the others. The creation of unity is merely assumed by consciousness, in this latter case[81].

Both of these viewpoints, of the soul being either simple or composite, come from the error, one from error of sensation and the other from the error of intellect. And the root of all this errors is the assumption that the soul or personality exists. Charles Robert Anon heteronym formulates this in this passage of the utmost significance:

---

[81] Ibid

> Notice that the real notion of my emotion centralized, seems to be, in the mind, the notion of the centre as cause, the notion of myself as Cause. Here then is the true, the real Cause of the pseudo idea of Free-Will: the transmutation of the act of the emotions which are mine into the acts of myself. True, my self is my emotions, centralized, but in emotions is the basis of myself and not in the centralization them.
> If my emotions be decentralized, as happens in instinctive acts, in customary acts, in sleep, in a state of hypnosis- still they can act. **But a centralization, in itself, is an abstraction, is nothing.** The emotions are the principal things. The centralization of nothing is nothing[82].

What Pessoa is trying to say, is that we have thoughts, we have sensation, we have emotions, yet our person, our ego, our self is nowhere to be found, because it is an assumption of the mind. Self is the centralization of thoughts and emotions, and because centralization is an abstraction, then it is nothing, which means that Self does not exist, hence there is no one, who can will, and no free will. It is easier to understand this with analogy. Let's say there are three oranges on the table, the oranges they are real, like thoughts and emotions, yet the number three does not exist in nature, it is creation of the

[82] Ibid

mind, and as such it has no reality under itself. That is why Caeiro says about Nature:

> I saw that there is no Nature,
> That Nature doesn't exist,
> That there are hills, valleys and plains,
> That there are trees, flowers and grass,
> That there are rivers and stones,
> But that there is no whole to which all this belongs,
> That a true and real ensemble
> Is a disease of our own ideas.
> Nature is parts without a whole.
> This is perhaps the mystery they speak of[83].

There is only that, which exists, hills, plains, flowers, trees, stones. The nature, as a whole, is just a disease of our ideas, and does not exist. Similarly, our Self does not exist, it is an abstraction of the mind, which is the result of our education. This is the meaning of the Campos words in Tabacaria:

> I am nothing.
> I'll never be anything.
> I couldn't want to be something.
> Apart from that, I have in me
> all the dreams in the world.

In fact Campos has a separate poem «I am nothing»:

> I am nothing, do nothing, follow nothing,

---

[83] Caeiro. «Keeper of the sheep» XLVII

Deluded, I bring my being along with me.
I do not understand understanding, or know,
Being nothing, if I must be what I will become.

In another poem Campos says: «I'm beginning to know myself. I don't exist». Caeiro calls it a «Great Secret» and a «Great Mystery». Charles Anon even further details importance of this:

> It is urgent for me here to point importance of this principle. **It is the basis of the human, too human, dogmas of the immortality of the soul, of its freedom, of its perfect simplicity.** The stupendous realization of an abstraction which consists in elevating out a mere centralization of emotions, which has a reality by them and in them, and only in so far as they are there all centralized, in elevating this into a reality, into personality — this is the lowly and feeble basis of the most rooted dogmas, of many and many of the most transcendent speculations[84].

This is the basis of human condition, the core individual belief that it exists as a real entity, that's the root of all dogmas. The goal of Christianity is salvation of the soul (ego), which simply is an illusion that disappears with death, hence there is nothing to save, but realize that "I and the Father am One".

---

[84] Nuno Ribeiro. Pessoa Philosophical Essays: A Critical Edition

Similarly, psychology provides help recipes to fix the psyche, which does not exist:

> Besides the refutation, by the search for origins, of these traditional dogmas, this principle — not to say, this discovery — gives us a new method in the science of psychology. Psychology ceases to treat and to consider the individual soul, very naturally, because this does not exist.[85]

Soares also writes:

> Today I was struck by an absurd but valid sensation. I realized, in an inner flash, that I'm no one. Absolutely no one. In that flash, what I'd supposed was a city proved to be a barren plain, and the sinister light that showed me myself revealed no sky above. Before the world existed, I was deprived of the power to be. If I was reincarnated, it was without myself, without my I[86].

When you realize that the ego self does not exist, then comes the understanding that all there is is just the sensation and that is what you are:

> In these languid and empty hours, a sadness felt by my entire being rises from my soul to my mind — a bitter awareness that everything is a sensation of mine and at the same time

---

[85] Ibid

[86] Pessoa. Book of Disquite, 262. Translated by R.Zenith.

> something external, something not in my power to change[87].

Pessoa is saying that he himself is just one of his sensations. And since Campos, unlike Caeiro, was living in the city, he identified himself with the city, Lisbon, its streets, trams, tobacco shop:

> Walking on these streets, until the night falls, my life feels to me like the life they have. By day they're full of meaningless activity; by night they're full of a meaningless lack of it. By day I am nothing, and by night I am I. There is no difference between me and these streets, save they being streets and I a soul, which perhaps is irrelevant when we consider the essence of things. There is an equal, abstract destiny for men and for things; both have an equally indifferent designation in the algebra of the world's mystery[88].
>
> I'm tired of the street, but no, I'm not tired of it — the street is all of life. There's the tavern opposite, which I can see if I look over my right shoulder, and there are the piled-up crates, which I can see by looking over my left shoulder; and in the middle, which I can only see if I turn around completely, there's the steady sound of the shoemaker's hammer, at the entrance to the offices of the Africa Company. I don't know what's on the upper

---

87 Ibid 3

88 Ibid 3

> floors. On the third floor there's a rooming house which is said to be immoral, but so it is with everything, life.
> Tired of the street? Only thinking makes me tired. When I look at the street, or feel it, then I don't think: I do my work with great inner repose, ensconced in my corner, bookkeepingly nobody. I have no soul, nobody here does — it's all just work in this large office[89].

This is the «religion of myself»:

> Today I'm an ascetic in my religion of myself. A cup of coffee, a cigarette and my dreams can substitute quite well for the universe and its stars, for work, love, and even beauty and glory. I need virtually no stimulants. I have opium enough in my soul[90].

And if the main sensation of Caeiro is seeing, the one for Campos is smelling. «The sense of smell is like the strange way of seeing» says Soares. And in particular, it is the smell of cigarette:

> Then I lean back in the chair
> And keep smoking.
> As long as Destiny permits, I'll keep smoking

---

[89] Ibid 379

[90] Ibid 251

ALCHEMIST BERNARDO SOARES: «OTHERS DO NOT EXIST»

Bernardo Soares resembles Alvaro de Campos and is the author of the «Book of disquiet», a «factless autobiography» of Pessoa himself. That is why a lot of his notes apply to his heteronyms as well. Soares was always preoccupied with the question of other being:

> One of my constant preoccupations is to understand how other people can exist, how there can be souls that aren't mine, consciousnesses that have nothing to do with my own, which — because it's a consciousness — seems to me like the only one. I accept that the man standing before me, who speaks with words like mine and gesticulates as I do or could do, is in some sense my fellow creature. But so are the figures from illustrations that fill my imagination, the characters I meet in novels, and the dramatic personae that move on stage through the actors who represent them[91].

Soares understands rationally that «a man is a living being just like me», but for him, like for any other person, «everything that isn't my soul is no more for me than scenery and decoration»:

> I feel more kinship and intimacy with certain characters described in books and certain

[91] Pessoa. Book of Disquite, 317. Translated by R.Zenith.

> images I've seen in prints than I feel with many so-called real people, who are of that metaphysical insignificance known as flesh and blood. And «flesh and blood' in fact describes them rather well: they're like chunks of meat displayed in the window of a butcher's, dead things bleeding as if they were alive, shanks and **cutlets of Destiny**[92].

Soares summarizes: «A human creature, as far as I'm concerned, has no soul». Other men are basically automaton:

> From birth to death, man is the slave of the same external dimension that rules animals. Throughout his life he doesn't live, he vegetatively thrives, with greater intensity and complexity than an animal. He's guided by norms without knowing that they guide him or even that they exist, and all his ideas, feelings and acts are unconscious — not because there's no consciousness in them but because there aren't two consciousnesses[93].

Others are not just «chunks of meat» and «cutlets of Destiny». «Vegetative thriving» indicates, that Soares likened others to vegetables, that have «less importance than a tree», as well.

---

[92] Ibid 317

[93] Ibid 150

> But since their true life is vegetative, their sufferings come and go without touching their soul, and they live a life that can be compared only to that of a man with a toothache who won a fortune — the genuine good fortune of living unawares, the greatest gift granted by the gods, for it is the gift of being like them, superior just as they are (albeit in a different fashion) to happiness and pain. That's why, in spite of everything, I love them all. My dear vegetables![94]

Soares with Campos are two sides of the same coin. So when Campos proclaimed «I am nothing», Soares makes the next step by concluding that «others do not exist»:

> No, others don't exist... It's for me that this heavy-winged sunset lingers, its colours hard and hazy. It's for me that the great river shimmers below the sunset, even if I can't see it flow. It's for me that this square was built overlooking the river, whose waters are now rising. Was the cashier of the tobacco shop buried today in the common grave? Then the sun isn't setting for him today. But because I think this, and against my will, it has also stopped setting for me[95].

The tragedy of other beings is nothing other than

---

[94] Ibid 313

[95] Ibid 317

«scenery»:

> That's why I've always seen human events — the great collective tragedies of history or of what we make of history — as colourful friezes, with no soul in the figures that appear there. I've never thought twice about anything tragic that has happened in China. It's just scenery in the distance, even if painted with blood and disease.[96]

Pessoa is an «empty stage» where this scenery takes place. His heteronyms are, thus, the same part of the scenery as the real people.

> I've created various personalities within. I constantly create personalities. Each of my dreams, as soon as I start dreaming it, is immediately incarnated in another person, who is then the one dreaming it, and not I.
>
> To create, I've destroyed myself. I've so externalized myself on the inside that I don't exist there except externally. I'm the empty stage where various actors act out various plays[97].

Empty stage has the same connotation as the image of the «bottom of the well» staring at the stars. Soares says: «Stepping back from myself, I see that I'm the bottom of a well». Another image used by Soares is that of a photographic

[96] Ibid 165

[97] Ibid 299

plate:

> I'm an ultrasensitive photographic plate. All details are engraved in me out of all proportion to any possible whole. The plate fills up with nothing but me. The outer world that I see is pure sensation. I never forget that I feel[98].

Another utilized image is similar to bottom of the well is the «corner of the dance-hall»:

> The man in the corner of the dance-hall dances with all the dancers. He sees everything, and because he sees everything, he lives everything. Since everything is ultimately our own sensation, to have actual contact with a body counts for no more than seeing it or just remembering it[99].

When you are dancing, you are dancing with one person, when you are in the corner, you are dancing with all the dancers. To dance with everyone, you do not need to touch. Since touching is one of the sensations, of which seeing is the most noble, it is enough just to see everything inside yourself, without getting close:

> Seeing and hearing are the only noble things in life. The other senses are plebeian and carnal. The only aristocracy is never to touch. Avoid getting close — that's true nobility[100].

---

98 Pessoa. Book of Disquite. Translated by R.Zenith

99 Ibid 373

Soares is saying that «all humanity's social existence lies before my eyes». «I passed by, I saw, and — unlike them — I conquered. Because my victory consisted in seeing».

[100] Ibid 427

MASTER ALBERTO CAEIRO: «I AM THE SIZE OF WHAT I SEE»

Pessoa was a master of poetic koan-like formulas describing the stages of nondual awareness. Baron of Teive starts the path of stopping the mind with his «where intelligence exists, life is impossible». When internal dialog stops, Pessoa comes to realization that «there is no reality but sensation» and Ricardo Reis realizes that life is just a «sensual passing of time in moments». Then awareness from senses turns to itself, asking the question of «who am I», and Alvaro de Campos formulates the only possible true answer, that «I am nothing». This is the meaning of Greek «know thyself». If I am nothing, then Soares makes the next logical step, stating that «others do not exist». In the end, after realization that ego does not exist, yet we observe the whole world, the question is raised in mind, what is it that we see.

And finally master Alberto Caeiro formulates the answer, that it can not be anything other than me, «I am the size of what I see». The true self, the observer, which is behind anything, is everything. This is a shocking realization, that everything we see is ourselves. And Bernardo Soares describes how that happened in «Book of

Disquite»:

> I experience a feeling of inspiration and liberation as I passively reread those simple lines by Caeiro that tell what naturally results from the smallness of his village. Since it is small, he says, there one can see more of the world than in the city, and so his village is larger than the city...
>
> Because I'm the size of what I see
> And not the size of my stature.
>
> Lines like these, which seem to spring into being on their own, independently of whoever says them, cleanse me of all the metaphysics that I automatically tack on to life. After reading them, I step over to my window overlooking the narrow street, I look at the immense sky and the countless stars, and I'm free, with a winged splendour whose fluttering sends a shiver throughout my body.
>
> «I'm the size of what I see!» Each time I think on this phrase with all my nerves, the more it seems destined to redesign the whole starry universe[101].

Soares explains that these lines «cleanse him of all metaphysics». This means that it cleanses him of all mind speculations and all assumption made by the intelligence of the ego, including the largest assumption of it all, that our selves (souls) actually exist. Caeiro poetically puts this

---

[101] Pessoa. Book of Disquite. 46. Translated by R.Zenith

anti metaphysics also in the following way:

> The mirror reflects rightly;
> it does not err because it does not think.
> To think is essentially to err.
> To err is essentially to be blind and deaf

If I am nothing, then everything, what I see is what I am. And when Soares steps over to his window to look at the immense sky and countless stars, he realizes with «all his nerves» that he is looking at himself, at his true self and not at the ego self.

Another Pessoa zen-like analogy is the likening of the true self to shepherd. When the true self observes the world as itself as if it was shepherd, then everything it looks at in the world basically become his own thoughts, and it is looking at them as shepherd is looking at the sheep. When I was the «size of my stature» or the «size of my height» that means that my self was in the body limited by my body's height and all the things were outside of me. But when I became a «size of what I see» or as Greeks put it «a measure of all things», then everything including stars in the sky are now inside my true self. That is the meaning of the poem «Keeper of the sheep» :

> I'm a keeper of sheep.
> The sheep are my thoughts
> And my thoughts are all sensations.

I think with my eyes and ears
And with my hands and feet
And with my nose and mouth.
To think a flower is to see it and smell it
And to eat a fruit is to know its meaning.
So on a hot day
When I feel sad at so enjoying it,
And stretch full-length on the grass,
Closing my hot eyes,
I feel my whole body lying in reality,
I know the truth and I'm happy[102].

Once again, the main problem is the existence of ego with its constant internal dialogue and thought process, which sinks the True Self into the illusion of what is not, instead of focusing on what actually is in front of our eyes, because that is the only thing that IS:

The essential thing is to know how to
Knowing how to see without thinking,
Know when to see,
And don't even think when you see
Not even see when you think.
But this (sad of us who bring the clothed soul!)
It requires deep study,
A learning to unlearn

Caeiro using revoking once more the sunflower image:

My gaze is clear like a sunflower.
I believe in the world as in a daisy,
Because I see it.

---

[102] Caeiro Keeper of the Sheep IX

But I don't think about it[103]

In a different poem Caeiro elaborates that «thinking is not understanding» and if you look at the nature without thinking, it does not mean you do not understand it.

My gaze is clear like a sunflower.
I take to roaming the roads
Looking to my right and to my left,
And now and then looking back...
And what I see all the time
Is something I had never seen before,
And I am very good at realising that...
I know how to have the same essential wonder
That a child has if, at birth,
He could notice he's really been born...
I feel I'm being born every moment
Into the eternal newness of the world...
I believe in the world as in a daisy
Because I see it.
But I don't think about it
Because thinking is not understanding...
The world was not made for us to think about
(Thinking is a sickness of the eyes)
But to look at it and agree...
I have no philosophy: I have senses...
If I speak of Nature it's not because
I know what it is,
But because I love it, and that's why I love it,
For whoever loves never knows what he loves
Nor why he loves, nor what loving is...
Loving is eternal innocence,

---

[103] Ibid XXIV

> And the only innocence is not to think[104].

Caeiro says that he has no philosophy anymore, but he is enjoying his senses, content with his senses. Campos was recalling:

> And I suddenly asked my master Caeiro, «Are you content with yourself?» And he answered, «No: I'm content'. It was like the voice of the earth, which is everything and nobody[105].

There is no self, just content, and that is the content of what IS:

> The amazing reality of things
> Is my everyday discovery.
> Each thing is what it is.
> How can I explain to anyone how much
> I rejoice over this, and find it enough?
> To be whole, it is enough to exist.
> I have written quite a number of poems
> And may write many more, of course.
> Each poem of mine explains it,
> Though all my poems are different,
> Because each thing that exists is always proclaiming it.
> Sometimes I busy myself with watching a stone,
> I don't begin thinking whether it feels.
> I don't force myself to call it my sister,
> But I enjoy it because of its being a stone,

---

104 Ibid II

105 A. Cardiello, B. Ryan, G. Tusa. Fernando Pessoa and Philosophy

I enjoy it because it feels nothing,
I enjoy it because it is not at all related to me.
At times I also hear the wind blow by
And find that merely to hear the wind blow makes
it worth having been born.
I don't know what others will think who read this;
But I find it must be good because I think it without effort,
And without the idea of others hearing me think,
Because I think it without thoughts,
Because I say it as my words say it.
Once they called me a materialist poet
And I admired myself because I never thought
That I might be called by any name at all.
I am not even a poet: I see.
If what I write has any value, it is not I who am valuable.
The value is there, in my verses.
All this has nothing whatever to do with any will of mine[106].

Caeiro «just knows the truth and is happy». He does not need any external stimulants, he «has enough opium in his soul».

Unlike Campos, who was the poet of the city, Caeiro was the poet of nature. And like Pessoa,

---

106 Caeiro. Discontinuous Poems

who founded sensationism, Caeiro was the founder of neo-paganism. Pessoa said that Caeiro's work was «the reconstruction of paganisms», that even Greeks or Romans were not able to do:

> Paganism is the one religion that springs directly from nature, that's **born from the earth**, from attributing to each object its true reality[107].

Attribution to each object its true reality means recognizing oneself in that object, seeing object as your own thought, seeing oneself in Nature, true paganism.

The Nature is what exists in present moment, since the past and future do not exist. Every moment is, thus, perceived as new, fresh, nature creating itself in the present. This is «the eternal newness (novelty) of the world» in the present moment:

> Live, you say, in the present.
> Live only in the present.
> But I don't want the present, I want reality.
> I want the things that exist, not the time that measures them.
> What is the present?

---

[107] A. Cardiello, B. Ryan, G. Tusa. Fernando Pessoa and Philosophy

It's something in relation to the past and the future.
It's something that exists by virtue of other things existing.
I want only reality, the things themselves, without any present.
I don't want to include time in my awareness of what exists.
I don't want to think of things as being in the present; I want
to think of them as things.
I don't want to separate them from themselves, calling them present[108].

[108] Caeiro. Assorted poems. From R. Zenith A little larger than universe.

PESSOA KEYS

WESTERN PHILOSOPHY

The main question of philosophy is the question of knowledge, how subject knows the object. We are born with mind in the «blank state», tabula rasa, as Locke called it, without rules of processing the data. These rules come to us from the cultural dogmas and life experiences and intend to create in individual a «common sense», which is a sound, practical judgment concerning everyday matters. The «common sense» stems from naive realism, which was summarized by Lee Ross, as the conviction that we see the world as it is and that when other people see it differently, it is they that do not see the world for what it is. The common sense worldview is that of a dualistic perception, meaning that objects are different from subject.

The child initially has direct perception without mental concepts. If a child sees a red side of red-green ball, then, when the ball rolls behind the wall and comes back with its green side, the child thinks it's two different balls. Later in the process of his upbringing he is able to keep objects in mind and create their different variants, learns the concepts of the sphere and creates an indirect logical chain, which helps him identify it as one ball. David Hume writes:

> Of these impressions or ideas of the memory we form a **kind of system**, comprehending whatever we remember to have been present, either to our internal perception or senses; and every particular of that system, joined to the present impressions, we are pleased to call a **reality**.[109]

This is obviously a necessary process for individual development. Yet, as a result of this learning process and getting exposed to different biases and dogmas the creation of the unique individual identity takes place. These multiple mental concepts create a «kind of system», «network of beliefs», that forms human ego.

The basis of this «network of beliefs» is common sense and naive realism: 2+2 =4, dog has four legs, earth rotates around the sun, e=mc2. The existence of atoms is also a mental concept, since a layman cannot really percept it, but just learns it from the pictures of textbooks. Willard Quine writes in «Two dogmas of

---

[109] D. Hume. Treatise on human nature

empiricism»:

> For my part I do, qua lay physicist, believe in physical objects and not in Homer's gods; and I consider it a scientific error to believe otherwise. **But in point of epistemological footing the physical objects and the gods of Homer differ only in degree and not in kind. Bo**th sorts of entities enter our conception only as cultural posits. The myth of physical objects is epistemologically superior to most in that it has proved more efficacious than other myths as a device for working a manageable structure into the flux of experience[110].

Holding a belief in atoms from the point of view of mind is really no different from belief in gods of Homer. It does not matter if the belief is true or false, as long as it helps that individual live its life. Different people basically create different narratives or live through «alternative movies» in their head (according to Scott Adams). When two individuals argue, we observe the clash of two independent networks or models of reality given to us through our perception. When people learn, they add new nodes to their belief network. If people loose the argument, they just re-evaluate their network and rearrange those conceptual nodes. There is a difference though

---

110 W. Quine Two dogmas of empiricism

between center and periphery (edges) of the network. People usually adjust their periphery, yet the core of beliefs remains unchanged, no matter how much proof can be given. Religious fanatics, that live in a totally different mental reality, are a good example of that. Willard Quine further says:

> The totality of our so-called knowledge or beliefs, from the most casual matters of geography and history to the profoundest laws of atomic physics or even of pure mathematics and logic, is a man-made fabric, which impinges on experience only along the edges. Or, to change the figure, total science is like a field of force whose boundary conditions are experience. A conflict with experience at the periphery occasions readjustments in the interior of the field. Truth values have to be redistributed over some of our statements. Re-evaluation of some statements entails re-evaluation of others, because of their logical interconnections — the logical laws being in turn simply certain further statements of the system, certain further elements of the field. Having re-evaluated one statement we must re-evaluate some others, whether they be statements logically connected with the first or whether they be the statements of logical connections themselves. But the total field is so undetermined by its boundary conditions, experience, that there is much latitude of choice as to what statements to re-evaluate in the light of any single contrary experience. No

> particular experiences are linked with any particular statements in the interior of the field, except indirectly through considerations of equilibrium affecting the field as a whole[111].

Once again, at the core of this «network of beliefs» lays the belief in the ego. As Descartes said: «I think, therefore I am». This constant thinking in the subject is a result of constant internal dialogue. This ego thrives on the parasitical mental concepts, and, as such, is a concept itself. It is either dreaming about the future or remembering the past, never living in the present moment. That is why Baron of Teive proclaims: «Where intelligence exists, life is impossible». Thus, ego lives in illusions and is illusion itself. In order to truly live in present moment, ego must be annihilated. This is exactly what Pessoa realized as his greatest discovery. The idea of «self» is idea of centralization of thoughts and emotions, and as such, in itself it is an abstraction, and thus it is nothing. Self does not exist. «I am nothing», exclaims Alvaro de Campos. This is the same as Hume's bundle theory of self, which is just a collection of properties (thoughts and emotions) bound together:

---

[111] Ibid

> I may venture to affirm of the rest of mankind, that they are nothing but a bundle or collection of different perceptions, which succeed each other with an inconceivable rapidity, and are in a perpetual flux and movement[112].

The layman belief is that object is different from subject, body is different from mind. This is Cartesian dualism expounded by Descartes, which is at the root of modern Western worldview. Merleau-Ponty in «The Visible and the Invisible» writes:

> We see the things in themselves, the world is what we see: formulae of this kind express a faith common to the natural man and the philosopher — the moment he opens his eyes; they refer to a deep-seated set of mute «opinions» implicated in our lives. But what is strange about this faith is that if we seek to articulate it into theses or statements, if we ask ourselves what is this we, what seeing is, and what thing or world is, we enter into a labyrinth of difficulties and contradictions[113].

David Hume in the ««Treatise on human nature» summarizes it the following way:

> Now it is evident, that, whatever may be our philosophical opinion, colors, sounds, heat and

---

112 D. Hume. Treatise on human nature

113 Merleau-Ponty. The Visible and the Invisible

> cold, as far as appears to the senses, exist after the same manner with motion and solidity, and that the difference we make between them in this respect, arises not from the mere perception. So strong the prejudice for the distinct continued existence of the former qualities, that when the contrary opinion is advanced by modern philosophers, people imagine they can almost refute it from their feeling and experience, and that their very senses contradict this philosophy[114].

By modern philosophers at the time Hume meant Berkley, who, a few decades after Descartes, challenged this worldview in his «Principles of human knowledge»:

> It is indeed widely believed that all perceptible objects — houses, mountains, rivers, and so on — really exist independently of being perceived by the understanding. But however widely and confidently this belief may be held, anyone who has the courage to challenge it will — if I'm not mistaken — see that it involves an obvious contradiction. For what are houses, mountains, rivers etc. but things we perceive by sense? And what do we perceive besides our own ideas or sensations?[115]

The object does not exist independently of our

---

[114] D. Hume. Treatise on human nature

[115] Berkley. Principles of human knowledge

perception, and since we perceive everything through our mind, everything is mind. «Everything is a sensation», proclaims Pessoa.

Getting back to the main question of philosophy, we see that subject does not exist and object does not exist, so the only thing left is perception itself. Once again, phenomenologist Merleau-Ponty in «The Visible and the Invisible» summarizes it best:

> Precisely because, in what is most proper to me, **I am nothing**, nothing ever separates me from myself, but also nothing draws my attention to myself, and I am in ecstasy in the things. ... it is the **same thing to be nothing and to inhabit the world**; between the knowledge of self and the knowledge of the world there is no longer any debate over even ideal priority. In particular the world is no longer *founded on* the «I think,» as the bound on the binding. What I «am» I am only at a distance, yonder, in this body, this personage, these thoughts, which I push before myself and which are only my least remote distances and conversely I adhere to this world which is not me as closely as to myself, in a sense it is only the prolongation of my body — I am justified in saying that **I am in the world**.[116]

When «I am nothing», then «I am in ecstasy in

[116] Merleau-Ponty. The Visible and the Invisible

the things». Ecstasy means being «outside of oneself». One of the illusions of naive realism is the identification with the body as the border between subject (ego) and the object (world). The realization of «I am nothing» results in the breaking through this border, a person literally becomes «outside of oneself», identifying with pure perception of what it sees at the moment. «I am the world», says Merleau-Ponty as a result of such experience, but before him Pessoa already pronounced: «I am the size of what I see».

CHRISTIANITY

«Thy Kingdom come», says Christ in the Lords Prayer, then he continues «the kingdom of God is come unto you» (Mt 12:28). Kingdom of God means «so that God may be all in all» (1 Cor 15:28), while «all in all» means «That they all may be one; as thou, Father, art in me, and I in thee, that they also may be one in us» (Jn 17:21). The fact that «kingdom of heaven has come near» (Mt 4:17) is the «good news» (Gospel), that was preached.

But in order to enter the Kingdom of God one has to be «born from above»: «Jesus answered and said unto him, Verily, verily, I say unto thee, Except a man be born again, he cannot see the kingdom of God» (Jn 3:3). «Birth from above» implies the death of that, which is below: «You fool! What you sow does not come to life unless it dies» (1 Cor 15:36). «For whoever wants to save their soul will lose it» (Mt 16:25). What must die is the «old self»: «put off your old self, which is being corrupted by its deceitful desires» (Eph 4:22). «Put to death, therefore, whatever belongs to your earthly nature: sexual immorality, impurity, lust, evil desires and greed, which is idolatry» (Col 3:5). «I die daily», says apostle Paul (1 Cor 15:31).

The death of the «old self» and birth of the «new self» (Col 3:10) in practice means a transformative change of mind or metanoia in Greek, which was incorrectly rendered as repentance. This change of mind does not consist in constant regret of old sins and deeds, but in «coming to senses», turning of mind to its Farther, instead of feeding in duality illusion with pigs (Parable of Prodigal Son) and nondual realization that «I and the Father am one» (Jn 10:30). «Here there is no Greek and Jew, circumcised and uncircumcised, barbarian and Scythian, slave and free; but Christ is all, and in all» (Col 3:11). The last saying clearly indicates that in Christ there is no duality of «Greek and Jew», «slave and free». Similarly, Maximus the Confessor writes that the man has to overcome in the deification process the duality pairs: created and uncreated, intelligible and sensible, heaven and earth, paradise and universe, male and female (Ambiguum 41, also in Quaest. ad. Thal. 48, 63).

The dualistic worldview is the result of the Fall, when man tasted the fruit from the «Tree of Knowledge of Good and Evil». This is a state of developed ego of Kain, whose progeny had scattered and created a developed civilization, yet the ego has to be slain, like Abel for the realization of union with God. The state of nonduality is a worldview of children, which do not have a developed ego. «Verily I say unto you, except ye be converted, and become as little children, ye shall not enter into the kingdom of heaven» (Mt 18:3). The children's worldview implies observing the world as is, in the moment without mental judgment, stopping internal dialogue, which again stems from duality. «Where intelligence exists, life is impossible» says the Baron of Teive.

When the mind stops, this is the «peace of God, which passeth all understanding» (Phil 4:7). But for adult to arrive to this worldview one must undertake a radical mental transformation that results in the destruction of the ««network of beliefs» that constitutes its ego and in realization that his old self is an illusion and does not exist. This is the realization of Campos «I am nothing». This is death of ego of which Christ says: «Whoever wants to be my disciple must deny themselves and take up their cross and follow me» (Mt 16:25).

After collapsing or extinction of self, one realizes that all the accumulated knowledge including science and religion is nothing, it's an illusion of mind, and he himself is «nothing but dust and ashes» (Gen 18:27). All the rich inner world is nothing for God. «For the wisdom of this world is foolishness with God» (1 Cor 3:19), and that is why «blessed are poor in spirit» (Mt 5:3).

The fact, that there is no subject, means that one can identify self in anything that he sees. The centralization inside the body disappears and the mind can shift its center on any object, be it a table or a lamp, and look at the body as if from that object, from the side, so to speak. The mind then does not know if it is in the body or outside the body. This is the state of ecstasy or being «outside of oneself». Apostle Paul called it «third heaven»: «I know a man in Christ who fourteen years ago was caught up to the third heaven. Whether it was in the body or out of the body I do not know — God knows» (2 Cor 12:2).

This is «kingdom of Heaven». In this state body feels inanimate, like any other object (table or lamp) and no different from them. This is «always bearing about in the body the deadness of the Lord Jesus» (2 Cor 4:10). This is the crucifixion of flesh, it feels like dead body hanging on the mind: «they that are Christ's have crucified the flesh with the affections and lusts» (Gal 5:24). When the mind is detached from the body, it feels like the body was shed, and, as a result, there is a feeling of lightness: «For my yoke is easy, and my burden is light» (Mt 11:30). Once you recognize, that it is ultimate Truth, it also feels like ultimate freedom. «Ye shall know the truth, and the truth shall make you free» (Jn 8:32). This also gives the filling of Bliss, which was supposed to be experienced in Paradise.

After the death of ego mind comes out of one's head and fills all the visible space, every object feels like Self inside that space (mind). There is no subject object dichotomy. You do not need to go to the mountain, the mountain is inside you. Mountain throws itself into the sea of mind (Mk 11:23). This is the «mind of Christ» (1 Cor 2:16). Campos said «I have in me all the dreams in the world» and Caeiro exclaimed «I am the size of what I see»! Merleau-Ponty said: «I am the World». There is only what one sees, the concepts of mind do not exist. And what one sees, is his own Self, there is only that what is, the Perfection, the Paradise. «Consider the lilies of the field, how they grow; they toil not, neither do they spin. And yet I say unto you, That even Solomon in all his glory was not arrayed like one of these» (Mt 6:28—29). «The kingdom of God is within you» (Lk 17:21).

In the reflections on unity with God Pessoa distinguishes three types of Consciousness: Individual, World and Divine. The individual consciousness means that Subject has created itself in particular small object (body) its own subject (ego) and became conscious of itself in a very limited way. One has to make this ego infinitesimal (extinguished) in order for Subject to become identical with Object (infinite world) that one sees. This is World Consciousness or Being (the mind of Christ). Then this state gets annulled and one returns to its original state of Divine Consciousness, where there is no subject, nor object. This is the state of Non-being (Father, whom no one seen «except the Son» (Mt 11:27)). Pessoa writes in that regard that «the abstraction of Reality is Being, the abstraction of Consciousness is Non-being». In the state of nondual awareness, everything becomes clear all at once, and the mind realizes that «I am the Father are one».

SOCRATES

In his last dialogue, Phaedo, Socrates defines philosophy as the practice of dying. He says:

> True philosophers practice dying, and death is less terrible to them than to any other men. Consider it in this way. They are in every way hostile to the body and they desire to have the soul apart by itself alone. (67e)

Similarly a few paragraphs before he defines the state of being dead as «the state in which the body is separated from the soul and exists alone by itself and the soul is separated from the body and exists alone by itself» (64e). So, death, then, is the separation of soul and body, when the body is alone by itself and, similarly, the soul is alone by itself[117]. He does not say, though, that the body has to be actually dead for that purpose.

In reality, it is possible to separate soul and body while both of them are alive, and this is the true practice of true philosophers. The outcome of this practice is essentially the experience of «Third Heaven», described previously, when apostle Paul was in the state of «whether in the body or apart from the body». In that state of nondual awareness the body is alone by itself, as

[117] David Ebrey. The Asceticism of the Phaedo: Pleasure, Purification, and the Soul's Proper Activity

if an inanimate object and experienced as no different from any other external object. And the soul is alone by itself, outside of body, «caught up to paradise and hearing inexpressible things, things that no one is permitted to tell». Socrates describes it the following way:

> When soul inquires alone by itself, it departs into the realm of the pure, the everlasting, the immortal and the changeless, and being akin to these it dwells always with them whenever it is by itself and is not hindered, and it has rest from its wanderings and remains always the same and unchanging with the changeless, since it is in communion therewith. And this state of the soul is called wisdom. (79d)

The word philosopher translates as «lover of wisdom", thus to acquire wisdom, he must practice dying. When the soul is separated from the body and is alone by itself, it identifies with the «World Spirit» as Hegel puts it. It is the realization of «I am That» (tat tvam asi) or «I and the Father am One». The question then is what is the soul in its attachment to the body, and the answer is – it is ego. The ego is that, what must die in the practice of philosophy. Socrates on multiple occasions identifies body with prison:

> Soul is fastened and welded to the body and is compelled to regard realities through the body as through prison bars, not with its own

> unhindered vision, and is wallowing in utter ignorance. And philosophy sees that the most dreadful thing about the imprisonment is the fact that it is caused by the lusts of the flesh, so that the prisoner is the chief assistant in his own imprisonment. (82e)

In 83d Socrates adds, that «each pleasure or pain nails it as with a nail to the body and rivets it on and makes it corporeal». While immersed in the body, soul sees everything through ego, like "through the glass darkly" (1 Cor 13:12) or like in the Plato's cave. So, if the soul alone in itself is identical to God, which in all traditions including Greek is symbolized by bull, then its junction with body through pleasure and pain, that is ego, is essentially a bull human chimera, a Minotaur, that is locked in the body-prison-labyrinth and which has to be slain to set the soul free.

In this regard, it is interesting to note that the setting of Phaedo is essentially that of the myth of Theseus and Minotaur, living in the cave labyrinth[118]. The dialogue starts with the explanation that Socrates death is delayed because of Athenian religious holiday celebrating Theseus killing Minotaur, which

[118] D. Futter. Myth of Theseus in Plato's Phaedo

prohibits the killing during that time. Socrates himself represents both Theseus and the Minotaur. It is mentioned that, while in prison-labyrinth, right before drinking poison he was «staring like a bull» (117b). Also, similarly to Theseus, travelling with «seven pairs» of young people consisting of nine males and five females to be sacrificed, Socrates in prison was surrounded with nine Athenians and five foreigners (59b). By killing himself Socrates, similarly to Christ, represented Priest and Sacrifice at the same time. As his final words he compares poison to libation, which was also a form of religious sacrifice: «What do you say about pouring a libation to some deity from this cup? May I, or not?» (117b).

If Socrates is Theseus then there is the question of who is his beloved Ariadne. Dylan Futter suggests that it could be Phaedo himself, who excludes himself of the fourteen guests that he counted. In this case, the thread of Ariadne, that allows soul to escape body-labyrinth, is the Socrates dialogue itself. The purpose of this last dialogue with Phaedo is to overcome the fear of death, to «save them and himself» (58b). The fear of death is what keeps us in the matrix, since illusory ego is constantly trying to survive to prolong its existence. Cebes in Phaedo compares fear of death with hoblogoblin:

> Cebes laughed and said, "Assume that we have that fear, Socrates, and try to convince us; or rather, do not assume that we are afraid, but perhaps there is a child within us, who has such fears. Let us try to persuade him not to fear death as if it were a hobgoblin."

The Greek word used for hoblogoblin is mormolykeia, which means a "wolf like creature". Greeks used it as synonym of bugbear or bogeyman, a bear like demon. Minotaur, which is a bull human creature, can similarly represent this "fear of death". It is said that Socrates drank poison «very cheerfully and quietly» (117c), meaning that he overcame the fear of death, killing Minotaur inside. To do it for others Socrates says that he would have to «sing charms to him (Cebes) every day until you charm away his fear (of death)» (77e). The Greek word for charm used by Socrates is actually epoide or incantation. Cebes asks Socrates: "how shall we find a good singer of such charms, since you are leaving us?" (78a). Socrates, thus, is a singer of charms or enchanter, like a magician, or sorcerer who casts spells to destroy the illusion of fear of death. And that charm or spell is the Phaedo dialogue itself.

YOGA AND ADVAITA

This is the explanation of Yoga. Yoga is not about stopping the mind, as it is not possible to stop the modifications (vritti) of mind (citta), even when you are in Samadhi. Yoga is about stopping the association of your true Self with the modifications of your mind. The association of Self with modifications of the mind creates the illusion (maya) of the second self, and, thus, we get two birds sitting on the branch of the tree. As RigVeda describes it: «Two birds associated together, and mutual friends, take refuge in the same tree; one of them eats the sweet fig (Jiva); the other (Atman) abstaining from food, merely looks on».

There are no chakras, at least the way they are described in the books, as different types of lotuses, letters, gods and colors associated with them. Whoever describes them in great detail and recommends their visualization, has no clue about Yoga and Samadhi. There are jolts of energy from tailbone to the head crown preceding the awakening, which could be verbally described as serpent power kundalini, the rest of the details about left and right channels (ida and pingala) and five types of prana are all made up.

Lower or savicalpa types of Samadhi result from activation of what can be called ajna chakra or the «third eye of Siva». In reality it is a gaze through the forehead accompanied by a strenuous feeling in the middle of the forehead between two eyes. This feeling can be experienced from squinting of the eyes, hence all the recommendation in Bhagavad Gita about «fixing the gaze between the eyebrows», yet you can squint your eyes all day long and never achieve Samadhi.

Once you direct that activated gaze on any external object, you can identify yourself with that object. There is no subject and object anymore, the duality is destroyed, this is nondual awareness. That is why Siva is called the destroyer of illusion (maya), when you look with that gaze it destroys the duality. To illustrate the illusion of duality, Shankara uses famous «snake rope analogy». When at night looking from a distance one can mistaken a rope for the snake, but after looking more carefully one recognizes the rope. There are no two objects — snake and rope, there is only one object rope. But when one sees the snake, the rope disappears, and vice versa. Similarly, when looking with regular pair of eyes one sees object separate from subject, but when looking with the «third» eye, duality disappears and one sees object as self (subject).

This is accompanied by feelings of bliss (ananda samadhi) and true Self (asmita Samadhi). You can identify yourself with any object and also see your body as the object like any other, without any internal life of the ego, as if dead inside.

You still have awareness of Self, although there is no more ego, hence it is savicalpa Samadhi. At the next step, you realize that you are nothing, just black void, for a second you loose consciousness of Self as well, this is death or nirvicalpa Samadhi. After that, the mind breaks through the crown of the head and expands filling all the visible space (this can be described as activation of sahasrara chakra). Now all the space you see you identify with your new resurrected Self and you understand that your body is walking inside your own self, as if a dead object among other objects. When you realize that you are everywhere, this is omnipresence. You have a feeling that now you know everything there is to know about reality, this is omniscience. Since there is only one Self and there is no one else, there is no one that can hurt you and you experience feeling of omnipotence. That's when you understand that

Atman is Brahman, tat tvam asi. This is the end of Yoga.

This is the explanation of Raja Yoga. This term was used by Vivekananda specifically for the four higher steps of ashtanga yoga described in Patanjali's Yoga-Sutras. There are different ways to extinguish ego and realize no-self. Bhakti-yoga is the devotion to God until a person forgets his ego. Karma-yoga is selfless action based on duty. Jnana-yoga is a philosophical enquiry into subject-object. Raja-yoga provides specific eight steps of achieving nondual awareness, although the first four steps in reality are not essential, despite the claims otherwise. Whoever claims, that one has to give up on meat or restrain his sexual energy, else he will never achieve higher states of consciousness, has never really experienced those states himself and just quotes ancient texts.

Pranayama or a specific way of breathing does assist in realization of higher states. The only requirement there is that the breath must be slow, with inhalation slowly transitioning to exhalation (for dharana) and exhalation gradually turning into inhalation (for dhyana). The breath does not disappear in Samadhi, but becomes unnoticeable.

Pratyahara is considered to be the control of the senses, that they are withdrawn from their objects into the mind (like turtle withdraws its limbs). In reality, it is realization of the fact that objects are not real and whatever we experience is all happening in our mind through the senses. «There is no reality but sensation» as Pessoa proclaimed. For example, when we look at the lamp, we have to understand that the picture, that we see in our retina is essentially flat, volume is the illusion that is created within our mind. We can touch the lamp and feel cold and hard surface or the burning of the bulb. The temperature and texture are then associated by the mind with the visual representation of the lamp. We can smell the dust burning on the bulb. On the other hand, we should also be aware that at the same time a dog or a bat will have a totally different experience of this same picture.

When describing pratyahara, Vivekananda says that the best way to practice it, is to sit still and let the mind go, observing all its crazy thoughts and ideas, jumping around like a monkey, without being attached to them. This attitude is similar to Ricardo Reis's «I let the life pass me by». It is for this reason, since pratyahara precedes the other higher states, we have placed

Reis, as a mystic, before other heteronyms.

Continuing the exploration of object in such manner, we focus mind on it and this is called dharana or concentration. Patanjali calls this state of mind «single pointedness» (ekagrata). In reality, this is realization of the fact that since everything is happening in the mind, then this object of concentration does not really exist. The continuation of «single pointedness» is the next step called dhyana or meditation. In reality, while exploring the illusory nature of object during dharana, the person starts exploring himself, coming to realization that he is not his body, his emotions, his thoughts, but then realizing that his ego is also an illusion, an abstraction, and as such it does not exist. «I am nothing» says Campos. Thus, during dharana we realize that object does not exist, during dhyana we loose our self in the process, realizing that subject does not exist either, which raises the question of «Who am I». And the answer to that question is Samadhi, or realization of Oneness, nondual awareness, identification of subject and object, that I am that.

Patanjali unites last three steps, dharana, dhyana and Samadhi into samyama. And, depending on where one directs samyama, he gets the answer to different questions. If it's a regular material object, then one achieves vitarka samadhi, if it is a mental object, then vicara Samadhi. Focusing on the object and seeing that object as self means that you can also look at your own body as if from that object, from the side. This is the state of ecstasy and one experiences the feeling of bliss (ananda Samadhi), as the mind is experiencing detachment from the body and attachment to the object. Focusing samyama inside the body also leads to the feeling of destruction of the ego and realization that the true I is not the ego, this is asmita Samadhi. All this comes from activation of ajna chakra and is also called samprajnata Samadhi. During the asamprajnata Samadhi the seer (Purusa, observer, witness) completely identifies with the seen (Prakriti, which is cognitive, moral, psychological, emotional, sensorial and physical aspects of reality). The mind breaks through the head and spills all over the seen space. «I am the size of what I see», exclaims Caiero. «I have in me all the dreams of the world». This is the state of entasy, when everything is inside the Self. Purusa understands that there is only it, this is the state of «aloneness» (kaivalya).

Advaita Vedanta identifies four states of consciousness, three of them are experienced by regular men: the waking state, where the consciousness is operating in physical body, the dreaming state in subtle body and the deep sleep with causal body. The underlying state is pure consciousness, Turya, the state of nondual awareness, where knowledge, the knower, the known becomes one. Pessoa identifies the first three states as different dimensions, and humans live in those different dimensions or «facets of ourselves». He writes in the «Book of disquiet»:

> Perhaps it will be discovered that what we call **God**, so obviously on a plane beyond logic and space-time reality, is one of our modes of existence, a sensation of ourselves in another dimension of being. This seems to me perfectly possible. Perhaps **dreams** are yet another dimension in which we live, or perhaps they're a cross between two dimensions. As our **body** lives in length, in breadth and in height, it may be that our dreams live in the ideal, in the ego and in space — in space through their visible representation, in the ideal through their non-material essence, and in the ego through their personal dimension as something intimately ours. The **ego** itself, the I in each one of us, is perhaps a divine dimension. All of this is complex and will no doubt be determined in its time. Today's dreamers are perhaps the great precursors of the ultimate science of the future. Of course I don't believe in an ultimate

> science of the future, but that's beside the point[119]

In this abstract Pessoa identifies three levels of hierarchy — ideal, ego and space. Body lives in space, dreams live in ideal, the ego («I in each of us») is God. This goes back to three paths of magicians, mystics and gnostics. Life is the journey of the mind through these states of waking, dream and sleep:

> Life is an experimental journey that we make involuntarily. It is a journey of the mind through matter, and since it is the mind that journeys, that is where we live[120].

Most of the people lose their self-awareness in these states. Pessoa through practice of imagination has shifted his consciousness center from waking state to the dream state, in which case waking state becomes just one of the dreams:

> I'm almost convinced that I'm never awake. I'm not sure if I'm not in fact dreaming when I live, and living when I dream, or if dreaming and living are for me intersected, intermingled things that together form my conscious self.[121]

---

119 Pessoa. Book of Disquite. 76. Translated by R.Zenith

120 Ibid 373

121 Ibid 285

Even the difference between dream and sleep is blurred:

> I don't sleep. I interexist. A few vestiges of consciousness persist. I feel the weight of slumber but not of unconsciousness. I don't exist. The wind... I wake up and go back to sleep without yet having slept. There's a landscape of loud and indistinct sound beyond which I'm a stranger to myself. I cautiously delight in the possibility of sleeping. I really do sleep, but don't know if I'm sleeping.[122]

Elsewhere, Pessoa said, that «Nature is the difference between the soul and God». Again, nature is a waking state, soul is a dream state, while sleep without dreams is God:

> Sleep is fusion with God, Nirvana, however it be called. Sleep is the slow analysis of sensations, whether used as an atomic science of the soul or left to doze like a music of our will, a slow anagram of monotony[123].

Compared to the fourth state, Turya, the state of consciousness, underlying those states, these three states are just an illusion (Maya). And, assuming that state of consciousness is the true life and that, which gives life to other states, then those three states are death compared to the

---

[122] Ibid 281

[123] Ibid 155

fourth state. While immersed in the wake state we think that this is where the life is, but once we transition to the state of true consciousness, this waking state becomes death. Pessoa writes about that:

> We are death. What we call life is the slumber of our real life, the death of what we really are. The dead are born, they don't die. The worlds are switched around in our eyes. We're dead when we think we're living; we start living when we die.
>
> The relation that exists between sleep and life is the same that exists between what we call life and what we call death. We're sleeping, and this life is a dream, not in a metaphorical or poetic sense, but in a very real sense.
>
> Everything in our activities that we hold to be superior participates in death and is death. What are ideals but an admission that life is worthless? What is art but the negation of life? A statue is a dead body, chiselled to capture death in incorruptible matter. Pleasure itself, which seems to be an immersion in life, is in fact an immersion in ourselves, a destruction of the relations between us and life, an excited shadow of death.[124]

With respect to this state the whole world is an

---

[124] Ibid 178

illusion on the surface of feelings:

> Often enough the surface and illusion catch me, their prey, and I feel like a man. Then I'm happy to be in the world, and my life is transparent. I float. And it gives me pleasure to get my paycheque and go home. I feel the weather without seeing it, and there's some organic sensation that pleases me. If I contemplate, I don't think. On these days I'm particularly fond of gardens.[125]

Those, who experience the fourth state, Turya, become Jivanmukta or Liberated. This doctrine was also used in Theosophy, so Pessoa was very familiar with it. This experience was described in «Book of Disquiet»:

> I'm older than Time and Space because I'm conscious. Things derive from me; all of Nature is the firstborn of my sensations.[126]

Once he realized who he was as consciousness, he went back to his waking state, which is the state of sleep or death, compared to Turya:

> It was just a moment, and I saw myself. I can no longer even say what I was. And now I'm sleepy, because I think — I don't know why — that the meaning of it all is to sleep.[127]

---

[125] Ibid 67

[126] Ibid 218

[127] Ibid 39

Jivanmukta is the one who have also reached Kaivalya, that is the state of aloneness or solitude. This state Pessoa expressed in the following way:

> Suddenly I'm all alone in the world. I see all this from the summit of a mental rooftop. I'm alone in the world. To see is to be distant. To see clearly is to halt. To analyze is to be foreign.[128]

The consequence of realization of nonduality is the awareness, that there is only One and there is nothing else, and as such you are alone. Being alone is somewhat boring, hence Pessoa constantly writes about existential tedium:

> Tedium, yes, is boredom with the world, the nagging discomfort of living, the weariness of having lived; tedium is indeed the carnal sensation of endless emptiness of things. But tedium, even more than all that, is a boredom with other worlds, whether real or imaginary; the discomfort of having to keep living, albeit as someone else in some other way, in some other world; weariness not only of yesterday and today but also of tomorrow and of eternity, if such exists, or of nothingness, if that's what eternity is. It's not only the emptiness of things and living beings that troubles the soul afflicted by tedium, it's also the emptiness of the very soul that feels this

[128] Ibid 83

> vacuum, that feels itself to be this vacuum, and that within this vacuum is nauseated and repelled by its own self.[129]

Generally, people overcome tedium of their everyday lives by traveling, but Pessoa most of his life spent in Lisbon, and did not travel anywhere, partly because of the events unfolding in his imagination:

> Travel? One need only exist to travel. I go from day to day, as from station to station, in the train of my body or my destiny, leaning out over the streets and squares, over people's faces and gestures, always the same and always different, just like scenery.
> If I imagine, I see. What more do I do when I travel? Only extreme poverty of the imagination justifies having to travel to feel. [130]

Pessoa overcomes the tedium with the help of his imagination, which plays the most important part of his inner life.

> In the countries that others go to, they go as anonymous foreigners. In the countries I've visited, I've been not only the secret pleasure of the unknown traveller, but also the majesty of the reigning king, the indigenous people and their culture, and the entire history of the nation and its neighbours. I saw every

---

[129] Ibid 381

[130] Ibid 451

> landscape and every house because they were me, made in God from the substance of my imagination[131].

Pessoa considers reality as an «episode of the imagination» since everything is made from the «substance of my imagination»:

> In Madrid, Berlin, Persia, China, and at the North or South Pole, where would I be but in myself, and in my particular type of sensations?[132]

---

[131] Ibid 138

[132] Ibid 451

ABOUT THE BOOK

Although the described stages can be intellectually comprehended, they are the actual transcendent states, which have to be experienced. It takes one to know one. And when someone had similar experiences they can easily recognize, if others had the same through some sort of resonance, although their own descriptions can be worded differently. This was my case with Pessoa.

While rambling around Tavira, I have stumbled upon a restaurant named “Alvaro de Campos”, having no clue, who Alvaro de Campos really was. On my way to the restroom I have noticed his quote, «I am nothing …», which is now used as an epigraph for this book. This quote stroke me, like a lightning, and the resonance with my own experiences have occurred. Digging later into Pessoa’s work resulted in unfolding of the vision, which is outlined in this book, confirming that the phenomenon of nondual awareness was behind Pessoa way of seeing things.

23.2.23 Cancun, Mexico

Made in the USA
Columbia, SC
05 May 2024

35296560R00072